Vision

Aligning with God's Purpose for your Life

J. L. Campbell

The Writers' Suite
St. Catherine, Jamaica

This book is a work of non-fiction. These accounts are from the author's perspective and memories, and as such, are represented as accurately and faithfully as possible. To maintain the anonymity of the individuals involved, some of the names and details have been changed.

Vision

Aligning with God's Purpose for your Life

J. L. Campbell

DEDICATION

To the father who loved me
The mother who raised me
The family that nurtured me
The community that sustained me
The husband who indulges me
The son who humors me
The tribe that supports me
The God who is moulding me
Into everything I am and will be.
My heart and soul are grateful.

ACKNOWLEDGEMENTS

I'd like to express gratitude to Ms. Shawn Williams of Women Of God Networking, who reminded Lissa Woodson (Naleighna Kai) of her vision to write a series of biblically based books that would speak to the hearts of people, especially women. In typical fashion, Naleighna Kai—developmental editor extraordinaire—moved swiftly to take this vision off the backburner.

During and after our discussion, I realized that I had much to say on the subject of purpose. Vision is not intended to diagnose or treat any mental conditions. I've written it to encourage those persons who may be focused on the negative, to shift recurring thought patterns onto a positive track.

Thanks also to my editor, Janice Allen, a woman of God, who unraveled my thoughts and made the reading of this book so much smoother. Debra Mitchell proofread the manuscript and provided timely and valuable feedback. Thank you! I'm also grateful to the other writers in this series, who are women of passion and purpose.

At the best and worst of times, I strive to remember that I can do all things through Christ who strengthens me.

J. L. Campbell

The cross she bears is not for the faint of heart. Her crown is no different. Storm clouds above her fill with preconceived notions and judgements from those who know nothing of her walk. Opinions fall like black rain, concealing the path while eroding her self-esteem for a time.

Happily, she thinks on Thee and tells the storm, You have no business here. My steps are ordered by The One that built the foundation of the world. I shall straighten my crown singed with trials and tribulations and face the dawn with wisdom and an overabundance of hope.

Just enough to rival the sun as she worships The Son.

—Stephanie M. Freeman,
author of *Necessary Evil* and *Unfinished Business*

"For I know the thoughts that I think toward you, says the LORD, thoughts of peace and not of evil, to give you a future and a hope."—Jeremiah 29:11

Face to Face With Reality

I'm a child of adultery.

My mother never kept it a secret. I had known for a long time, but not at a conscious level. Many times, she'd say, "Your father's wife …" in reference to one incident or another.

Yet, it was only a few years ago that I realized the significance of how I came to exist. At the time, I was thinking about my mother and our relationship. By then, fifteen years had passed since her death so it was way too late to find out more about how my parents found each other.

The most significant thing I remember about my father is how he loved me. He ran a hostel-type motel in downtown Kingston, and I'd visit him there. My memories of him are sketchy, but I cannot recall him ever speaking a harsh word in my hearing. He always sang Neil Diamond's "Sweet

Caroline" to me, which I never figured out because that was nowhere near my name. I guess it was one of his favorite songs.

I believe he was a serial cheater because aside from the two sons he had with his wife, he had me and another boy that I only saw once or twice. My father's wife was never unkind to me, but she wasn't kind either. Aside from greeting me with a sour expression, she had little to say to me. Now I understand why. Not only did she have to deal with the pain of a cheating husband, but he had the gall to thrust the result in her face.

From my mother's accounts, he was overprotective where I was concerned. Didn't want me visiting my grandmother in the country during the summertime because he thought she wouldn't have enough to feed me. Of course, my mother was outraged because this was her mother he was doubting.

My early years were filled with everything a child could possibly want or need. I was loved, spoiled a little—although my mother was a strict disciplinarian—but knew I was special to my parents. Somewhere along the line though, life intervened and I lost sight of that fact.

From time to time, I think about my mother's choices, which were at odds with some of the things she taught me. One of my earliest memories is of her teaching me the Our Father prayer. Despite the fact that I was but a tot, she expected me to memorize it. My evenings were traumatic because if I missed a few words, she took me to task, a few slaps being part of that deal.

Looking back, I realize she didn't know how to deal with the frustration she was going through in her situation, and some of that was transferred to me. As I still tell people, my mother beat me for *everything*. Thankfully, this stopped when I became a teenager, but we had verbal battles as I rebelled against what seemed to be the stranglehold she had on my life.

When my father died, I was devastated. At the time, I was twelve and in first form—grade seven—which is the age most children transition to high school in Jamaica. Naturally, our situation changed. No longer did we have the cushion of the financial support he provided. Thankfully, my mother, who was no sluggard, had gone into cosmetology.

In high school, morning devotion was part of our school life, whether we wanted to participate or not. I'm grateful for that now. So many of the hymns we sang have remained a constant in my life and now have even deeper meaning. At that time, I first came across a song based on Psalm 139 by American composer, Dan Schutte. The title is "Yahweh, I Know You Are Near."

David wrote that beautiful Psalm, which talks about God knowing us intimately. So much so, that while we were in the womb, before anyone else knew we were there, He knew.

Some years ago, I was talking to someone whose husband had had a child outside of their marriage. As she expressed her outrage and pain, I joined her in speaking unkind words about that child and her future. Later, I had a "come to Jesus" moment when I realized that the things I had said applied to my life since I came into the world the same way. I had to cancel all those words and ask my Heavenly Father for forgiveness.

The biggest take-away from that conversation was realizing that even when we can't see our purpose, God has a plan for every life. I can testify that I've never lost any opportunities or been deprived of any advantage because of how I arrived on planet Earth. David knew his Heavenly Father had chosen him, was with him every step of the way, and understood his every thought. In the same way, we should also be convinced that He chose us and is an ever present part of our journey, despite how we came into the world.

There's an interesting story in Judges 11 about a brave man, Jephthah, whose mother was a harlot, or prostitute, in today's terms. His father, Gilead, had a wife and other sons. When they became adults, they kicked Jephthah out of the house.

"You're not going to inherit anything that belongs to our father," they told him, "because you're the son of another woman."

Jephthah left home, fell in with some bad characters, and went about raiding with them. When war broke out between the people of Ammon and Israel, the elders of Gilead made a beeline to Tob, seeking Jephthah.

"We need your help fighting against the people of Ammon," they told him. "Come and be our commander."

"Hold on a minute now," Jephthah, might have said. "Weren't you the ones who kicked me to the curb? Did you not hate me and forced me to leave my father's house? Now you're in trouble, you come crawling to me to help you out?"

"Well, this is exactly why we need you," the elders said, as if nothing major had happened. "Come back with us, be the head over all the citizens of Gilead and help us fight this war."

"So let me understand this," Jephthah replied, hardly believing what he was hearing. "If I come and fight for you and the Lord gives me this victory, I will be your head?"

"Oh, yes, let the Lord witness between us if we don't keep our word."

Jephthah went home to Gilead with the elders, declared everything before the Lord, and was made the head and commander over the people. He set the king of the people of Ammon straight by giving the history of how the Isrealites came to own the land given to them by God. But he didn't listen, so they went to war over this land dispute. The Bible tells us in Judges 29, "Then the Spirit of the Lord came upon Jephthah ..."

He emerged victorious, but had to sacrifice his daughter because of the vow he made to the Lord. A first look at Jephthah would make us think he was a lost cause, being a bandit. Although he was rejected by his family and society, when the time came to rescue his people, Jephthah's boldness and skill made him ideal for the job. God knew that and put him in position to claim victory for His people.

One of the things I love about God is that He takes our circumstances, and the little we have, and makes much of them. Think about Jephthah's origins, his fall from grace through his actions, and where he ended up. In God's race, no matter where we start, He determines how we finish.

Consider this: Do you know in your soul that no matter how you made your debut on the stage of life, as David puts it, you are "fearfully *and* wonderfully made?" How would the lives of your family, friends, and associates be different if you weren't a part of their world?

Being A People Pleaser

By the time we became toddlers, we were conditioned to the words "good girl" or "good boy." Many of us never stop craving approval for as long as we live.

For most of my childhood years, my mother and I lived alone, so I spent a lot of time by myself. I wasn't lonely because I watched television and was a voracious reader. Books were my companions. Outside of novels, magazines, and comics, there was one neighbor my mother allowed me to visit. Venese—not her given name—was like a sister to me. We went on various outings together because if I had company, my mother was more likely to allow me to go.

School was one place where I was always looking for approval. I talked constantly. As one teacher told my mother, "Joy is the life of the party in class."

At the time, I felt betrayed by my English teacher. I mean, that was my best subject and how could she let me down like that? For the rest of my time in high school, my mother kept reminding me that I wasn't there to be a social butterfly. I was there to learn.

Of course, I wanted to please her, so I molded myself into what she wanted me to be. It didn't always work, but the chatterbox label didn't show up on my report again. I believe that incident, along with peer pressure and the need to fit in, helped to change my character.

Through the years, I've told people yes, when what I wanted to say was "No, I can't accommodate that." Or, I took on jobs knowing I couldn't deliver in as timely a manner as I would have liked. Some months ago, when I was feeling overwhelmed, I wanted to do a social media post to say something along the lines of, *If you ask me to help you, and I say I can assist in the short term, please do not believe me. I will be lying through my teeth.*

Being raised as an only child for most of my childhood years made me think I was selfish and mean because I'd never had to share anything. Even now, I prefer to purchase my own supplies. So at the office, I bring my own pens, highlighters, and other stationery, so I do not have to use what is provided by the work place.

The way I was raised helped me to teach my son to be conscious of other people's needs. But at some point, I missed the memo that I don't need to turn myself into a pretzel to help others.

Even today, I overextend myself to do favors for those who ask. I don't know how to pace myself, which means that I run projects—personal and otherwise—back to back, with no rest in between. Sometimes, this tendency to pack too many things into a day affects my ability to produce books according to the schedule I set for myself.

Before I was published, I was a member of a writing network.

One of my critique partners told me to never forget that my first responsibility is to myself. "Everybody else and everything can come after that," he said. "Work on your book first."

I've tried to remember this advice over the years, but I still slip. The result is that I grow overwhelmed when looking at all I need to accomplish. What usually brings my focus back is to simply stop, list what should be done, plus the order of their importance, and create an action plan.

No one understood the concept of saying "no" better than Jesus. He knew what He was here to do, said no to the distractions, ministered to the people who needed Him, and most importantly, made time to rest and commune with His Father.

Many of us, yours truly included, need lessons on how to set aside the many things that demand our attention and focus on ourselves. It's not selfish to say no because you need rest, time to recuperate, time to rejuvenate, or the space for self-care. Because most women are nurturers by nature, we run ourselves ragged taking care of the home and family, plus meeting the demands of the day job. Add in the requests for help that come from friends and relatives. However, the time often comes when we have to decide whether to say yes, to our detriment or say no, for our peace of mind.

The choice is yours and mine.

We weren't put here to drive ourselves to exhaustion. If Jesus told us He came that we may have life more abundantly, why do we think it's a badge of honor to keep going until we fall into bed at night so drained we can barely mumble a prayer before we sleep?

We cram so much into each day that we sometimes aren't able to enjoy our homes and families. When we lay in bed, our minds churn—like a hamster on steroids riding a wheel—figuring out how we're going to fill everybody's needs until we are beyond exhausted, yet we can't close our eyes.

The thing is, half the situations we think will go wrong, won't. And the people we are bending over backward to serve have options. They can either wait until it's convenient for us to do what they're asking, or find someone else to do it.

It's not sinful to think about our personal needs, or to take time for ourselves. If we're putting God first, fulfilling the needs of our family, then the myriad of things we do for work, friends, and associates later, that's the proper order.

Consider this: A wise person once said, "You can't pour from an empty cup." How different would your life look if you spent more time tending to your needs and saying no to things that do not serve you or fit into your lifestyle?

The Lord knows something we don't because He tells us to "fear not" 365 times in the Bible. That's one reminder for every day of the year. Think about the significance of that for a moment.

My first understanding of being the odd one out was some time between my fourth and sixth year. My biological sister was raised by a godparent—this is what I was told—and eventually, she came to live with my mother, my aunt, her daughter, and me. Another cousin, whose mother was abroad, also lived with us and was close in age to my sister. The two of them were usually up to something which my mother didn't approve of, so they were always in trouble.

Although I had a sitter, somehow my sister had the impression our mother brought her to Kingston to take care of me. At times, I was left with her and my older cousin. Their antics influenced and affected my life in ways that still exist today.

My family loved *Dark Shadows*, which starred Jonathan Frid in the role as Barnabas Collins. I suppose because there were half a dozen of us living in close proximity, it didn't occur to anyone to consider the effect a drama like that would have on me or my younger cousin. Fact was, I hated that show and would not even venture into the bedroom alone after watching it.

My sister and cousin knew I was terrified of that vampire. They encouraged a neighbor who lived in the same tenement yard—a property where different families live in rented spaces, but share bathroom and kitchen facilities—to take on the role of Barnabas Collins. Of course, all of this played out when my mother wasn't home.

Noel would put his hand inside his tee-shirt and shake the empty sleeve at me. In hindsight, I do not know why his pranks frightened me the way they did. Aside from the empty sleeve, he would make vampire teeth with the card insert from cigarette boxes. He'd cover it with foil. The effect of those silver vampire teeth made me hysterical.

So, they would lock me in an unrented room in the yard and he would do his vampire act through the broken window. I can't say they threatened me, but I don't know why I never told my mother. These experiences ushered the spirit of fear into my life. For many years, at the slightest provocation, I jumped at my shadow. Needless to say, I never became a fan of horror movies, nor did I enjoy the telling of ghost or "duppy" stories as we call them in Jamaica. When I did watch horror movies, I was never afraid that I'd have nightmares. I was more afraid of what might meet me in the dark at home.

Years later, I realized that my cousin really meant no harm. We had a conversation recently, in which I shared how that fear had followed me into adulthood and ruled my life for many years. She was shocked to know about the repercussions of their mischief.

"Are you serious?" she asked, sounding as if I had told her I'd robbed a bank. When I explained the effect of their actions, she apologized and stated what I knew. She never meant to harm.

The other day, I saw a video on Facebook of a little girl who was howling because some of the hair the women were using to braid their hair had attached to her foot. She tried to move away but, of course, the hair traveled with her. What was happening to her was a source of amusement to the women. They weren't mean, but watching that child have a meltdown brought back all that had been done to me when I was as small as she.

These experiences not only foster fear, but they can also plant a seed of rejection. While others are laughing and enjoying your discomfort, you may wonder what you ever did to deserve the treatment you received. Or why you didn't get the help and comfort no one thought to give. For many of us, the first place we meet rejection is in the home—even when it was done under the guise of fun. Then we go into the world and face negative responses from people who don't understand us, or who may be mean-spirited because it's simply who they are or who they've become because of how they have been treated.

Joseph's treatment from his brothers in the book of Genesis is quite different from what I went through. I wasn't thrown into a pit, nor was I sold into slavery, but what I saw as rejection from my cousin and sister impacted me on some level. If my mental well-being was of any importance, they wouldn't have thought it was okay to amuse themselves at my expense. And as we say in Jamaica, "What is joke to you, is death to me." I now know my sister didn't understand my mother, nor did she feel she was loved. I've never blamed her for taking out her resentment in the way she did. She simply thought our mother loved me more. I guess tormenting me gave her some measure of satisfaction.

In the intervening years, I buried most of the things I didn't want to face. As long as my early past didn't come to mind, there was no need to deal with the reason dread filled me over the smallest things. The reality hit that I was broken and why. God has been good to me, giving me a love of reading that has helped me to dissect my issues and better understand my personality.

Even now, I remind myself every so often that according to 1 John 4:18, *There is no fear in love. But perfect love drives out fear, because fear has to do with punishment. The one who fears is not made perfect in love.*

This verse has been a mantra when I've faced situations I was unable to handle. God was always there, and made a way for me. One night, I was in the shower and deathly afraid for no reason I could pinpoint. Jesus must have heard my desperate prayers because the Holy Spirit spoke a word into my spirit from Galatians 1:4. *I am delivered from the evils of this present world because it is the will of God.*

At the time, I'd never come across that verse, so I had to search on the Internet. Imagine my amazement to find that God loved me enough to whisper those words of comfort to my soul. That experience strengthened my faith and confirmed how much I meant to Him as a daughter. Even now, I'm blown away when that experience comes to mind.

Many years passed before I was delivered from the spirit of fear, but like every other aspect of our lives that do not serve us, it tries to come creeping back when I'm not vigilant. But I'm happy that God is on my side. With His help, I can "run through a troop and leap over walls." The Lord knows something we don't because He tells us to "fear not" 365 times in the Bible. That's one reminder for every day of the year. Think about the significance of that for a moment. I also take comfort in His word in Romans 8:31, which confirms that despite any form of rejection we face, "If God be for us, who can be against us?"

Consider this: We may face rejection, but the important thing is that God always has us close to His heart, even when we think we are on our own. He also knows exactly where He wants us to be at all times and gives us help precisely when we need it.

When Joseph revealed himself to his brothers during the famine, he said, "And God sent me before you to preserve a posterity for you in the earth, and to save your lives by a great deliverance. So now it was not you who sent me here, but God…"

"Write the vision and make it plain on tablets, that he may run who reads it. For the vision is yet for an appointed time. But at the end it will speak, and it will not lie. Though it tarries, wait for it; Because it will surely come, it will not tarry."

Habakkuk 2:2-3

Drifting Versus Strategic Planning

Romance swept into my life during my twentieth year. Before that, I was in 'serious like' with different guys. My mother was the kind of woman who would have killed me for even *thinking* about having a boyfriend, so that wasn't an option. Plus, it didn't occur to me that she didn't have more than two eyes and couldn't be everywhere at once.

That special young man made life fun and enjoyable. We were inseparable, and went on dates and trips with other people. For a time, everything was smooth and I was happy. Then came the shock when he announced that he was migrating to the United States. I wasn't the sort of person to make a big deal over the fact that he was going, but I knew I'd miss him.

For a while, we had a long-distance relationship. During that time, I changed jobs and went out with other friends, exploring the world and spreading my wings. Then the time came when

I realized that although he suggested that we get engaged, it probably wouldn't work. He was "fine" and I knew in my heart it was inevitable that he'd start seeing other people. Eventually, I suggested that we end the relationship. When I did, he told me that he never would have cut the cord if I hadn't.

What happened next made me realize how important it is to have a plan and vision for our lives. I drifted into another relationship because my boyfriend was no longer in the picture. With no direction in mind, I simply went with the tide, living from day to day. I fell in love, and married someone else. We did not start out struggling to build a future because he was a mature person who bought a home, and I ended up owning my mother's house. I've not had the experience, like many adults, of working hard to secure a permanent home.

The same approach crept into my writing life. I started in a good place. Full of energy and writing book after book because I was passionate about what I was doing. My energy lasted long enough for me to write thirty books, have six of them published through small publishers, and then something happened. It was as if I lost the zest to continue pushing and settled into doing lackluster launches that didn't serve me or my books. Previously, for each release, I came up with ideas specific to that book and a marketing plan.

We all want to be successful at what we do, but what do our actions say? Do we act as if we are ready for success, or duck down a side road and lay up in a comfortable place until we find the energy to get the next job done? I freely admit that I haven't been consistent with my goals. Sometimes, I've had to initiate a board of directors' meeting with God, plus me, myself, and I in attendance.

Half the time, we believe we can achieve our dreams on our own. Nothing is further from the truth. Not only do we need other people, we need firm plans—broken into small steps—and the humility to ask God for direction. Habakkuk 2:2-3 states it plainly. "Write the vision and make it plain on tablets, that he may run who reads it. For the vision is yet for an appointed time. But at the end it will speak, and it will not lie. Though it tarries, wait for it; Because it will surely come, it will not tarry."

Consider this: David was described as a man after God's heart. His life was a testament to God's faithfulness. He became what God ordained him to be. When he fell, he listened to God's messengers, repented, and got himself back in fellowship with his Father. Think about how different his life would have been if he hadn't followed God's direction and leading.

Do you believe you are walking in your purpose? How do you know you're on the right path? What does the evidence say?

"But as for you, you meant evil against me; but God meant it for good, in order to bring it about as it is this day, to save many people alive."

Genesis 50:20

Adjusting Your Expectations

Along the path of life, some of us make the unconscious decision to put aside our dreams. Disappointment piles upon disappointment, and we settle into a humdrum life, forgetting our childhood years when we had big visions. Whether it was the fun we were going to have at a family picnic or wanting Christmas to arrive so we could get our hands on all the gifts we asked our parents and Santa to deliver, our life was full of anticipation of good things to come.

Life has knocked us down often enough that we settle into doing what society dictates at each stage of our existence. After a while, our internal channel shifts from cherished aspirations to being in a holding pattern, and then to survival mode, or simply coping. Even our faith gets set to the side when we come upon circumstances that don't go our way. We accept our losses, but along with that comes the message that things don't always work out. So we should brush those mishaps aside, give thanks when things do pan out, and make the best of our situation.

There's a saying that our attitude determines our altitude. This is true, in part. Some things we have no control over—other people's reaction to us, their attitude and viewpoints, the way they do business. But what we *do* have control over is what happens in our minds and how we react to our challenges. It's easy to blame everything on other people and the things they do, but it makes more sense to think about how our own actions affect the resulting highs and lows.

In 1995, everything in my life went topsy-turvy. My husband lost his job and what followed was a succession of sales gigs that brought more stress than income. In the middle of all of that, our relationship changed, mainly because of his daughter's entry into our lives, plus the influence of her relatives.

We had a twelve-year-old girl who was resentful and difficult to deal with, which was confusing to me because she and I started out with a good relationship. She was A-okay while at our house during the weekdays. But a curious thing happened, in that whenever she spent the weekend with her mother's family, a different child returned.

I was not used to the acrimony and the cat-and-dog life, having been raised in a house where I grew up knowing I was loved. Many nights, I swung between hate and self-pity, while crying an ocean of tears. I loathed my husband for putting me in that position. His child had come into our lives because he asked me to take care of her. Before all the upheaval, I'd been insulated. In my mind, he'd taken me from my mother's home and thrust me into the tenth circle of hell.

Time passed and eventually his daughter moved out of our home. Truthfully, it was a relief. However, I didn't think about how the fractured relationship with his child affected my husband. I also didn't consider his feelings as his independence slipped away and he had to lean on me for financial support.

Not one bright spot stood out during that time. And as if that weren't bad enough, unexplained things that terrified me were happening around us. All I will say is that there was some supernatural activity involved, which is part of the Jamaican landscape. Eventually, I found out—through a circle of gifted prayer intercessors—that I had one foot in the grave. Only God's intervention prevented me from an early death.

I didn't believe we'd ever find our way out of the mire that engulfed us up to our necks. My world had tilted and everything familiar slid into a black hole. But my one constant was prayer. As grueling, protracted, and exhausting as that stretch of life seemed, we got past it and I believe my connection with the Heavenly One helped me stay sane.

Along the way, I've had to relearn to expect good things each day, to believe that God has my back, and that problems will work out. I think about Joseph's statement to his brothers (Genesis 50:20) after they sold him into slavery and he rescued them years later. He said, "But as for you, you meant evil against me; but God meant it for good, in order to bring it about as it is this day, to save many people alive."

We may wonder what we've done to deserve our current lot. We cry out in anger, self-pity, and despair, wondering where God is in our situation. That's part of what makes us human. Faith and the knowledge that we are here for a reason give us the courage to believe that we will win, despite our challenges.

Usain Bolt didn't arrive on the scene as the world's fastest man without discipline, hard work, injury, and setbacks. He persevered because he understood he was working toward a goal. We, too, must be mature enough to realize that if we stay the course, we will come out victorious, despite how dark our issues may seem. It's sensible to adjust our sails, based on what we see in the natural. But we should always believe that, like Joseph, we can survive the hardships life brings. He started out being ganged up on by his siblings, sold, lied on, then flung into prison, but ended up being elevated because he did what God ordained him to do.

The long walk is what builds character while we go through our trials. Joseph could have given up while imprisoned, especially after he accurately interpreted the dreams for the baker and butler. Imagine yourself appealing to Pharaoh's butler before he walks out of prison. "Whatever you do, don't forget about me. Put in a word for me with the king. I'm not sure how much longer I can make it in this place."

What does the chief butler do? He gains his freedom and forgets about Joseph. More than two years pass before that ingrate remembers him, and only because the Pharaoh had a dream no one could interpret.

The butler then had a flashback and remembered the promise he'd made to Joseph but hadn't kept, so he said, "I remember my faults this day …"

After Joseph was brought before the Pharaoh and correctly explained his vision, he was elevated and made second only to Egypt's ruler. Joseph was a teenager when he lost his freedom and was thirty by the time he came before the Pharaoh. I don't doubt that he had some days when he sank into the depths of despair, but he persevered. He looked forward to something better when he appealed to that butler to help get him out of his current condition.

As long as we're alive, we should believe there is better in our future. Troubles may pour over us like a flood but as we say in Jamaica, only salvation lasts forever. It is natural to adjust our approach when our plans don't quite go as we envisioned, but it is *not* okay to give up. God did not put us here to fail. The life lessons we learn on the way prepare us for the role and destination God has in our future.

Consider this: What dreams have you abandoned because the path to achieving them seemed too difficult? Does your situation look different now? What can you do today to increase your chances of succeeding in at least one area of your life?

Mental Strongholds

Joy, Joysie, Ms. Joy, and Joy to the World are among the names I've been called. We won't discuss the ones used to describe me when I was out of earshot. For the most part, my disposition has reflected my name. I like making people laugh and prefer to be in a good mood rather than in the doldrums, no matter what's going on in and around me.

Imagine my shock when I realized I'd become something of a pessimist without realizing it. My joy didn't erode overnight. Once upon a time, things occurred the way I needed them to happen. But I recently noticed that my mind has developed negative spaces. That was hard to accept. It's as if, because of my experiences, I now expect most things to be a hard slog. Even worse, I tend to become discouraged if things don't work out according to my timeline.

The irony is that I know there's a set time for all my prayers to be answered and difficult paths to be smoothed. Yet, I want it all now based on the here-and-now philosophy too many of us embrace because of the insta-society we live in. We want what we want now, as if our desires will come to us as quickly as microwave noodles or a pre-packaged dinner.

I understand that few things worth the effort are achieved without a struggle and nothing worth having comes easily. Yet, my mind is wired to expect instant gratification. When that doesn't happen, the "stinkin' thinkin'" sets in.

Subconsciously, I've learned to listen to the negative voice in my head that says, "Oh, well, it wouldn't have worked out anyway."

But I don't take the negative chatter lying down. When it surfaces, I announce, "That's not how it's going to go. I can do all things through Christ who strengthens me." Declaring positive things aloud gives them substance and settles the desired outcome in my mind. The word of God is powerful and we shouldn't lose sight of how our lives can be changed by speaking positively over our individual situation.

It's sometimes a struggle to act and speak positively when we don't feel like it. David was a man who fell into depression at certain points in his life. Psalm 22 shows us one of those instances. By the end of his lament, however, his equilibrium was restored through meditating and speaking about the goodness of God. Being a worshipper, he did what came naturally. He made a conscious decision to open his mouth and praise his Creator. In verse 25 and 26, David said, "My praise *shall* be of You in the great assembly ... The poor shall eat and be satisfied. Those who seek Him will praise the Lord."

Like David, we must grow to the point where we stir ourselves to open our mouths to declare God's goodness and proclaim what He created us to be. This requires that we learn to recognize when our thoughts don't line up with God's word and His promises to us. I can't tell you how many times I've been depressed for no good reason and the only thing that got me out from under it was thanking God for everything He's done in my life and speaking His promises.

A wise person once said the habits of a lifetime are hard to break. No truer words have been spoken, but with determination, we can take control of our mental life and encourage ourselves. None of this is easy. Prayer and worship can feel like work if you're not in the right frame of mind. But trust me, there is nothing that compares with feeling God's presence as His Holy Spirit speaks joy and peace to my soul.

Another truth I hold fast to is that God is the Master Builder. But how did he do it? "Let there be …" He spoke over creation and everything in the world fell perfectly in place at His command. The power of the spoken word is one of the most impactful lessons I've drawn from the Bible. In Job 22:26, after speaking about paying homage to God, Eliphaz says, "You will also declare a thing, and it will be established for you; So light will shine on your ways."

If God intended for us to be bogged down by our thoughts, emotions, and external struggles, He wouldn't have given us His Word and the instructions we need to change our situation. Challenge yourself to adjust the way you praise and worship. Use the mouth God gave you to love on Him. You won't regret the time spent adoring Him.

Consider this: David was in the doldrums when he asked *"Why are You so* far from helping Me, and from the words of My groaning?" He roused himself to worship and affirmed that he would praise God along with "all the families of the nations." If you are prone to negative thinking, can you remember when it first started and why? Picture how switching the channel in your mind and declaring uplifting words might change your current mood.

I invite you to declare positive words over your life this minute. Start by reminding yourself, "I am a child of The Most High God. I am blessed and highly favored. God's blessings will chase me down and overtake me. Gracious *is* the Lord and righteous; Yes, our God *is* merciful."

Charting Your Creative Path

Decision-making can be a struggle when you're multi-talented. God gives us ambitions and goals to help others and ourselves. The trouble is, sometimes we're so distracted by adversity and the challenges that we forget how truly gifted and talented we are.

We may start our journey focused on one discipline and find other areas of interest that challenge us. In my case, I tend to be a dilettante, which means I dabble in different things but really only have a superficial interest in them. So the cycle starts when I discover something I enjoy doing and I'm off and running. After my research, I'll spend a good deal of money, getting myself equipped for a new adventure. But something happens along the way. As soon as I achieve some level of mastery over what I'm doing, I lose interest and move on to the next thing. It has taken me some time to recognize this pattern of behavior.

Full disclosure: I don't know why I do this. What I can acknowledge is that I'm easily bored and when I am, it's on to another challenge. Or, I find another way to do what I'm currently involved in, to prevent boredom from setting in.

From a business standpoint, I'd say at some level I'm afraid of success. At the same time, I'm afraid of failure. I'm afraid that if I follow the path I'm on to the end, I might not do as well as I believe I should. This fear is likely what keeps me playing hopscotch with the things I enjoy, but never giving them my all.

The creative side of my life factors heavily into my day-to-day activities. At some point, my mind circles and lands on my current project and what needs to be done to complete it. Plus, there are the decisions on promotion and marketing. Creativity is like life. If we're not careful, we start out in one direction, then forget the original goal, and take side roads and paths not meant for us.

My development as a writer has included different genres. I've been fortunate in that whatever ideas I've put on the screen, I can make them work. I've developed friendships with readers who follow me in whichever direction my writing takes me,

Of course, there are paths I won't travel because I don't believe they fit my brand—even if I stand to flourish more than I currently do in terms of finances. I'm sure you've had to make similar decisions—whether they had to do with business ventures that didn't seem legit, or the folks you were involved with weren't your kind of people, or you realized that you would be throwing away money.

Intuition, business savvy, and communication with God will tell you when you're about to run into something that might not end well. My go-to recommendation is that pro and con list. If the negatives outweigh the positives, then I'm running in the opposite direction like Speedy Gonzales.

That's not to say that I haven't been bitten a time or two by bad decisions. Several years ago, I bought into an advertising campaign run by a writer with a large book club. Because the website looked good and the writer had been around for some time, I made the decision to invest US$180. That's $23,400 in Jamaican currency. What I didn't do was talk to any of my colleagues about whether they had any dealings with that business.

When my promotion date came and went, I reached out to the business owner. She assured me that my ad had gone here, there, and everywhere, including the mailboxes of her scads of book club members. To make a long story short, not even the crickets came to keep me company while I watched to see if the sales needle would shift.

I've learned much since then and try not to make a move until the Holy Spirit weighs in. Each of us has to learn to recognize when God is communicating with us. Otherwise, we'll run ahead, convinced we've heard from God, even when that isn't the case.

If you're hesitating, or doubt what you're hearing about the move you want to make, spend time in prayer until you have clarity. Don't make the mistake I did. The credit card company loved me for that misadventure, because I had to pay those fees without seeing any return on my investment. If I had done my homework properly and called that director's meeting with the Holy Spirit, I would have fared better.

Experience has taught me that when it's time, it's time. If God has directed the process and led you through it, nothing under Heaven and on Earth can prevent you from achieving what He has planned for you. Lean on Him for direction. He will never lead you astray.

Consider this: No matter what we do in life, it's important to consult with our Maker before going on a journey without a roadmap. As he psalmist noted, "Your word *is* a lamp to my feet and a light to my path."

He has our interest at heart. There is no decision so small that our Father wouldn't want to be involved. If we doubt what's being said, our guidebook for life is an excellent reference and aid to decision-making. Take heart in knowing that He cares about the large and small issues of your life. Seek Him as you make each decision. You'll never go wrong.

Deferred Dreams and Discouragement

Despite what we may think, we're responsible for our happiness. Joy, peace, and satisfaction can't come from our spouses, families, or friends. All of these gifts come from knowing who and whose we are.

The time will come when we have to reconcile the things we've done and neglected to do on this journey called life. Taking stock requires being honest about the things we believe are holding us back. Two of the biggest culprits are a lack of conviction that we can be successful at whatever we set our minds to, and thinking we don't have what we need to climb a seemingly unyielding mountain.

As hard as it seems, all we need to do is take that first step. Make an action plan and move on it. If we do nothing, we'll be stuck in the same place and later wonder how we ended up in a no man's land of stagnation. We'll think we didn't hear from God and that's why we never made a move, when in fact we were too terrified to even take a baby step.

We don't realize the importance of the mind and the role it plays in helping us meet our goals. I believe it's one of the most important tools we possess. Get your mind right and everything else follows. You can take a thought inventory this minute.

Do you believe you can achieve your dreams? Yes? No? Kinda-sorta?

If you don't believe you can, don't stress about it. You may be comfortable with your current situation, and that's all right.

What makes moving forward hard is the fact that we're not guaranteed immediate success. Some actors/writers/recording artists labored ten or even twenty years before becoming 'overnight successes'.

The public doesn't know about their struggle to stay on track—the self-doubt, fear, hard work, the urge to quit, the strength to get up one more time and continue after being knocked down again. They had to develop the will to exchange destructive mindsets for positive thoughts, as well as the energy to put one foot in front of the other when all seemed dark and there was no hope.

Remember, no one but you can achieve your uniquely-crafted dreams. The frustration you experience comes from letting discouragement make you give up on the things you were meant to do. If you choose to abandon your goals, you'll never know what you could have achieved. The story of the crossing to the Promised Land comes to mind.

God told Moses he was giving Canaan to the Israelites and asked him to send a team to scope out the land. A dozen men went, but only Caleb and Joshua came back with positive news. The others told tall tales about the land (it would swallow them up) and the people there (giants, who would defeat them). Their lack of conviction led God to allow them to wander through the wilderness for the next forty years. Only the men who told the truth and believed they could have taken Canaan lived to experience what God had promised. Don't let that be a reflection of your life.

Consider this: We can't see into the future, but we do have the capacity to plan and order our steps. Don't let another day go by without thinking about your dreams, needs, and purpose. Think about yourself for once. What makes you happy? Is there anything you wish to accomplish that you haven't tackled as yet? Do you see yourself starting the adventure that will make your vision a reality?

Processing Failure

I had a friend—now deceased—who was always starting businesses. By profession, Carl was a computer repairman, but he also ran a company canteen and a pet shop, put money into a courier company, and was involved in investing. Each time he shared what he was doing next, I marveled at his energy and his will to achieve whatever he set out to do.

That may be because my life has been mainly about working and writing. I've gone into several ventures but lost my mojo when things weren't going well. As is inevitable with creatives, I found other things to try. But, in the back of my mind, I counted those attempts as failures and something I wouldn't do again.

One day Carl and I were talking about the cake and pastry shop that my husband and I had closed because it wasn't sustainable, plus we weren't able to collect from some customers.

He said, "I treat everything as a learning experience. If I don't succeed at it now, then it's something that will help me at some point in the future."

That conversation gave me a different viewpoint. Still, I procrastinate over some decisions and don't treat business ideas with the urgency they deserve. It's as if I don't move because I'm afraid whatever I'm trying to do won't be an instant success.

The thing about life is that we are influenced by different people and make decisions based on a number of factors. We may reach for a variety of ideas in pursuit of success, but we are not guaranteed to make it big in all we try to do. If we were successful at everything we touched, our heads would likely be so big that they would break our necks.

Every lesson learned along the way is valuable. En route to whatever victories we have, we learn fortitude, patience, and skills we didn't possess before we launched into something new.

In January, my cousin called me and told me I was making cakes for a wedding. I said, "Hold on a minute, I'm not doing that anymore."

"Why not?" she asked.

I explained why we left that business. After putting in more than we were making over a sustained period, and not being able to collect on some jobs we had done, it was the best decision for us.

My cousin wasn't hearing that that chapter of my life was closed. "Well, you have to do this set of cakes."

"Why am I going to do that?" I asked.

She laughed, then said, "Because I'm getting married."

"Really? When?"

The date she gave me was less than a month away, but after we talked about it some more, I agreed to bake and decorate the cakes.

When I went shopping, the owners of the store and I had a long conversation. Nadine and her husband used to be neighbors of mine, so we were catching up since I hadn't seen them in some time. She was the person who taught me to make royal icing flowers. After giving her my list of items, I explained that I was only doing a favor for a relative and wasn't in business.

She shared an experience with me about a customer who owed her a significant balance on a wedding cake and still hadn't paid her years later. Her husband's contribution to the conversation was eye-opening. He said, "The burial ground is the richest place in Jamaica. So many dreams, goals, and visions are buried with those who never fulfilled the roles they were meant to play, nor pursued the dreams God put on their hearts."

His words caused me to pause and reflect.

I admitted that people's behavior should not have factored into our decision to close the business. A better approach would have been to try and tap into a new client base. Once God gives a dream, He will give the strength and make a way for it to come to fruition. As Nadine reminded me, "The world is waiting for your gift, but you are sitting on it because you allowed dishonest people to kill the desire God gave you."

Those words were good food for thought, which brings me to the next point. God did *not* create us to fail. His words tell us He knows the plans He has for us. If only we can grasp hold of our purpose and not let go of it, until we meet success. We only fail to thrive when we stray off the path He prepared for us.

Consider this: Have you ever wondered how Joseph felt when he was in prison for something he hadn't done? The lie his boss's wife told, that he tried to seduce her, was a serious one that changed the trajectory of his life. He could have been killed. Discouragement could have beset him after being left to languish in jail despite the promotion he had received because of his efficient service. God favored him, and the guard put Joseph in charge of the prisoners.

Joseph did that job with a spirit of excellence until the day he was summoned before the Pharaoh and was catapulted to greatness. Why not keep praying, praising, and expecting good things despite what life looks like now? There's nothing to lose and so much to gain.

The Relationship Between Consistency & Success

My writing journey began when I was twelve. Mills & Boon romances were my inspiration and I read them while in primary school. Of course, my teen years hadn't hit yet, but my mother didn't know I was reading that far above my age level. In high school, I penned romances that my classmates enjoyed. Then for years, my writing included only minutes of meetings and proposals. After a twenty-year break, I launched into fiction in my thirties.

I enjoyed renewing my relationship with the craft so much that by the time I was published, I already had a supply of completed books that only needed to be edited. My first publisher encouraged me to start a blog, which led me to become part of a vibrant blogging community that helped spread the word when my first book was released.

Over the next few years, I celebrated each release by doing a blog tour or some kind of blog hop that involved other writers. Hiring a tour company was out of the question because I couldn't afford the fees since I wasn't getting royalties every month as is the case with Amazon. The friendships I established helped me whenever a new book came out.

Success was important to me, so I did what was necessary to have a good launch. With each published book, I learned something new. When I became involved in boxed sets, I absorbed information about where to promote and the best places to advertise. I learned the value of being part of a community of women who had a vision to cop the number one spot in several categories. We divvied up the jobs among the writers according to their skill set. Of course, there was always that one person who disappeared when the work became intense and reappeared on release day when it was time to take a breather.

If I could cover all of those activities in one word, I'd say consistency. Even when I had personal challenges, I did my part because other people were depending on me.

But focus is also important, and somewhere along the way I changed gears and lost the drive and enthusiasm to promote each book in a way that would give it a good start on release day. My consistency level had slid off the chair, fallen under the table, and slinked away to hide.

Not showing up to put in the work means I'm not committed to meeting my goals. Discipline and determination are important, but I must honor the commitment to get to where I want to be—which is writing full time.

I've concluded that my efforts, all combined, to move me forward on my journey. Whatever worked for book one—and everything that contributed positively along the way and still works—is what I should be doing for book number thirty-eight. No excuses. No fooling myself. When we create a plan and tick off assignments as we accomplish them, we will have no doubt about the path we take to our definition of success. Also, we'll know exactly what worked and what didn't.

Consider this: What did David do consistently? He may have been a war machine, but aside from that, David prayed. David danced for God. David worshipped. He spent time with his Creator. This consistency in prayer is reflected in the Psalms he wrote and his exploits in the Bible. You don't produce that kind of intensity and beautiful sentiment without carving out time and putting in energy. What a wonderful example for us to follow in our walk with the Father, Son, and Holy Spirit.

Help Along The Way

Over the years, I've sometimes wondered if I'm on the right path in terms of my writing career. I've asked myself the question when the results I see don't match the efforts I've put in. I've looked over the fence many times and wondered if success had more to do with luck, talent, a great marketing team, or a combination of the three. Then I examined my biggest disadvantage: the inability to afford necessary services. The currency conversion between the U.S. and Jamaican dollars meant spending more than I could afford on my limited budget. Despite this, I'm thankful I didn't give up.

I've met many angels on this journey and I've also met some devils. I've come across people who don't understand themselves and why they are here. And there have been people who reminded me that I'm talented and should keep pushing.

Then there are those who never grow up. I've always believed in taking each person on their own merit, despite whatever they have going on. Amazed doesn't describe what I feel when people extend their bad feelings to include me, even though we've never spoken about their problem.

By accident, I discovered that someone on social media had unfriended and unfollowed me. Before that, I witnessed her ranting about people who canceled from her event to make her look bad. I did withdraw, but only because of financial reasons. A refund wasn't offered, nor did I ask for one.

Even then, I didn't understand what was happening. I can be really dense, but finally got the message when my book cover was excluded from a contest by this person who thought I had a grudge against her. When I realized what was going on, I withdrew myself from her reading group and counted it as another life lesson.

Since then, many opportunities have come my way and I've been fortunate to be among a group of wonderful women and men who give freely of their skills and talents. Despite how alone we feel at times, God always assigns people to take us where we need to be. He wouldn't give us dreams and aspirations if He didn't plan to help us achieve them.

Not only does He give us ability, He also finds people who will go out of their way to help our cause, sometimes without knowing why they're doing it. Even when we think we're stuck, as long as we acknowledge our dependence on Him, he pulls us out of the mud and sets us on our way again.

Whenever David landed in an insurmountable situation, God always found a way to either send him help or let him know he had walked into forbidden territory. And what happened next?

David was able to right the situations he'd made wrong, reconcile with God, and get back on the path to his destiny.

Sometimes we will be the ones who need to reach out for help. With some of us—myself included—that can be as difficult as pulling teeth. Just recently, I needed to buy some important items but had to ship them to the address of someone I know in Miami. That was a safer option than shipping direct to Jamaica. I'd just had several items delivered to his old address, but was reluctant to do so again a week later. Several days passed before I worked up the courage to ask. His response was, "No problem." Then he gave me his new address and told me to order the items.

If only I could get back the time I've wasted agonizing over asking for simple favors. I believe God put us here to serve each other, and I'm confident that isn't a rare attitude. I'm convinced God will move Heaven and Earth to get us to where He wants us to be. We must exercise our faith to believe He will supply our needs, through the vessels He provides.

Consider this: When famine came upon Egypt and the surrounding countries, Joseph's brothers went searching for food and survived through his generosity—despite the fact that they did him dirty. No matter if someone wronged us, we still extend a hand to help in a crisis.

How do you respond when God gives you an opportunity to help someone, especially if doing that favor will inconvenience you? Do you know you're the answer to someone's prayer for help? When was the last time you assisted someone without expecting anything in return?

"For God has not given us a spirit of fear, but of power and of love and of a sound mind."

2 Timothy 1:7

Anxiety ... The Big Fraud

It's Sunday morning and I'm sitting on a golf cart. We're in the open air and I'm with the tournament director, watching a group of players. A rules official is in the cart next to us, and we're all whispering because we don't want to disturb the group on the green. They putt out and walk away. I snap some pictures of the beautiful scenery and post them online. A moment later, I grab a newspaper and flip through it.

By now, my mind is churning. Because of COVID-19, we can't do a formal prize-giving but since a few of the prizes are on hand, we'll give those to the winners. I'm thinking about how to catch all the persons before they leave the course, then there's the matter of an email I needed to send. By now, I'm squirming because I want to be back in the clubhouse. Instead, I turn the page—yes, I'm still browsing the paper while all of this is going on in my mind—and there's an article about ten not-so-obvious signs that point to anxiety.

Something tells me to read, because of course, I suspect I've been dealing with a case the entire week. To my horror, I'm experiencing eight of the ten symptoms discussed. Especially when we have events, my anxiety level is out there in the stratosphere.

Jumping back to earlier in the week, I was wide-eyed each morning just before 4:00 a.m. Since I'm out of bed much too late each night, I value each moment of sleep. Waking up that early each day was my cue that God wanted to talk to me. I used the time, which served me well, because being grounded by prayer to meet the day is a good thing. During the tournament days, we worked for twelve hours and there were moments when I wasn't sure I'd make it. I was so tired. That same Sunday morning, when I woke just before four, I asked God why this continued to happen even on that final day. Yes, my question was a teeny bit petulant because my tail feathers were dragging after a whole week of waking up super early.

Before I finished asking, I received one word in my spirit: Preparation. At that point, I backtracked for obvious reasons. God knows all things best. Plus, there's the fact that if I hadn't been up praying every morning, I couldn't have made it through the week without His help. Aside from the administrative aspects, two of us were dealing with sixty-two other people in the competition. The scoring app was problematic for some, so that required interaction and finding solutions.

As I thought about the delivery of the message, Isaiah 65:24 came to mind. "It shall come to pass That before they call, I will answer; And while they are still speaking, I will hear."

That one-word answer to my query served as a reminder of how little I know, and how big God is. Then, seeing the article was a reminder of what I already knew. The nature of my job means I work with ten different executive members of a committee. Most, I don't hear from regularly. Others, more so. Being who I am, I prefer to do what is required for each person as soon as possible.

I'll be honest and say that sixty percent of the anxiety and stress I experience are self-induced. I've found ways of coping which include telling myself that I can only complete what is ordained for me to accomplish each day. Then there is the reminder in Philippians 4:6 to be anxious for nothing, but to let God's peace guard my mind through Christ.

In too many instances, I look back at major events and consider how I stressed over completing all related tasks. God was always there with reminders that I could do all things through Christ. His words say that despite everything, we can trust in Him and not lean on our own understanding. Half the time, it is because we give in to our worrisome thoughts that we become stressed and unable to cope efficiently. The kicker is that what we worry about never becomes reality.

When I become anxious, I try to remember these negative emotions are not from God. One of the verses I've come to rely on is from 2 Timothy 1:7 "For God has not given us a spirit of fear, but of power and of love and of a sound mind." If He hasn't given me fear, then He also hasn't given me anxiety. I know that for sure, and Proverbs 12:25 does say, "Anxiety in the heart of man causes depression, But a good word makes it glad."

Taming the mind is a form of discipline we *must* learn on our journey because it is possible to be led by our emotions to the point where we feel the sky is falling when nothing is further from the truth.

Consider this: How often have you fretted about a situation and spent days worrying only to experience a sense of anti-climax because the events you dreaded didn't materialize? This has happened to me all too often. If we stay occupied with imagined events, it's possible to miss the blessings and joy God provides each day.

When you next have an attack, remember that we can change *nothing* by worrying. It's simply one device the enemy uses to harass and distract us. Jesus asks in Matthew 6:27, "Which of you by worrying can add one cubit to his stature?" And if that's not enough food for thought, a great reminder comes from Psalm 94:19. "In the multitude of my anxieties within me, Your comforts delight my soul." There's nothing better than communing with God and knowing He is with us in our distress and provides peace for our troubled spirits.

Stirring the Gifts Inside You

If anybody asked what gifts and talents you have, what would you say? Maybe you'd think for a few seconds, then come up with hobbies you enjoy and are skilled at, or personality traits that describe who you are.

My view is that people are gifts presented to the world exactly as they are. Yes, you are a gift!

Do you brush off compliments about your personality or skills? If so, have you asked why? You may have convinced yourself that you have nothing significant to offer. Nothing could be further from the truth. Some believers are inclined to think they have to serve God in spectacular ways. This kind of thinking is erroneous. All God needs from us is our faith, attention, and obedience. Our assignment may be to encourage someone, lend a listening ear, or say a prayer. These small demands on our time lay the groundwork for us to do bigger things for Him in His appointed time.

You may have heard specific things prophesied over your life but have seen no evidence of them being manifested. No athlete ever moved to the top of their field without hard work, discipline, and sacrifice. Spending time with God will help you to distinguish His voice from the distractions around you. You will come to know when He has spoken on what He requires of you. When we are in tune with His instruction and leading, that's the time we can do much in His Kingdom.

We live in such a fast-paced world that it has become unnatural to sit and bask in silence. As women, we try to be everything to our family, friends, and associates. We give so much that we have little left to nourish ourselves. When we try to relax, we sometimes feel guilty for not being engaged in some productive activity. Yet, our minds and bodies aren't renewed unless we rest.

Half the time, I wake up tired because I didn't rest enough. Inevitably exhaustion creeps in each evening, the time I most enjoy reading the Bible and having a real conversation with my Maker. By then, my mind is too foggy to engage with Him meaningfully. I'm trying to do better by not allotting the very last part of my day to something so important to me.

While God loves us "with an everlasting love," I believe He is disappointed when we neglect sacred prayer time. Like any good parent, He wants to know about *all* the things that affect us. As David wrote, "You know my sitting down and my rising up; You understand my thought afar off." (Psalm 139:2). God knows every detail of our story, but wants to hear it from us. Too many times, we ask people to pray for us when God wants a direct line of communication with his hurting children. He wants to promote healing, show us support, and saturate us in His love, peace, and joy.

The most important conversations we have during our day are the ones with Him. We need His guidance and protection to start our day and move us through the things we cannot do on our own. Although we are self-reliant, He wants to be part of everything that affects us. No matter how small.

The most profound statement I have come across in recent times is from renowned Baptist preacher, Charles Spurgeon. "Rest time is not waste time. It is economy to gather fresh strength ... It is wisdom to take occasional furlough. In the long run, we shall do more by sometimes doing less."

God may be calling us to minister to others but we must be in good shape, praying, worshiping, covered by His blood, and equipped for spiritual battle.

The time between our calling and when we are active may seem excessively long. Decades may pass, but never doubt that God knows exactly what's needed to equip you for His purpose and the job only you can do.

While you wait, your responsibility is to work with the tools He gives you. Study the word, learn from the people He puts in your path, and stay obedient to Him. In due time, the Holy Spirit will teach you all that you need to know to fulfill your role on this earth. In 1 John 2:27, the writer puts it this way: "But the anointing which you have received from Him abides in you, and you do not need that anyone teach you; but as the same anointing teaches you concerning all things, and is true, and is not a lie, and just as it has taught you, you will abide in Him."

When I am tempted to get impatient, I remember Oswald Chambers' words. This Scottish evangelist and teacher's advice is for us to "Be patient and so utterly confident in God that you never question His ways or your waiting time."

Consider this: David's journey from the sheepfold to king over the house of Judah took time. God chose and anointed him while he was still a youth. David served King Saul, killed Goliath, went through various hardships, and fought many battles *before* he ascended to the throne. On his journey, he learned how to rule.

Think about what you've learned on the way to your career and the life you now have. Your knowledge and experience didn't come in a day, did they? Trust the process and believe God is still in charge of your destiny.

Surviving & Thriving Where God Places You

The other day, I read an inspirational message on social media that made me feel ungrateful. It said something to the effect that God does not have us in our current position because He can't do better, but that He strategically places us where we can do His will.

Although I work for a sporting organization, my day job is sometimes stressful. This is especially true when there are national teams traveling or we are hosting an international event. By the time I get home in the evenings, I am dead tired from the effort and intensity the preparation demands.

My position also involves different individuals. Most of them are great people to work with. Others, act as if they are demi-gods and are hard to collaborate with on projects. Many times, I want to quit. In fact, I already quit once and was subsequently asked to assist part-time, which I did. The person who became the head of the organization three months after I resigned, hired me to act as the administrator for a regional event, then re-hired me to the job I left. And yes, I received a significant pay increase.

Any job is easier when the boss trusts you and allows you to do the work you were hired to do. But when you have dreams and plans that go sideways because of the commitments that come with the day job, you question whether you're in the right position. Writing relaxes me, but when I can't write for a long while I become frustrated.

That message I mentioned earlier made me think. When we face problems, we tend to place limitations on God, forgetting what He has done in the past and all He's doing in the present. His word tells us that He's not a man that He should lie (Numbers 23:19), and we know Jesus speaks to us of believing and receiving.

The role we play is a gift, whether it is in our family or professional life. There is no one more suitable or better equipped for the position you are occupying than you. Even if you have doubts, based on what we know of God, He can equip us for positions for which we aren't qualified.

In 2005, our office moved to a different location. I took on the day-to-day responsibilities simply because administration is one of my strengths, and there was no one else to do it. Some months later, one of the directors advised that he wanted to second me—loaning an employee temporarily—to another company in the position of Operations Manager since I was already acting in the role. The other director with direct responsibility didn't want to do it. But God stepped in and I was appointed to the position. That lasted until 2010, when the facility changed hands and we relocated.

I had not been trained in running the operations side of that kind of business but God provided the right people to assist me when necessary. At least three persons who thought they were better able to do my job approached the directors. Despite that, I was never in danger of losing my employment. My record of efficiency and being a hard worker served me well.

In every task I was expected to do, I asked God for success in getting it done. I'm not certain I would take on anything within that scope again, but I was confident that God would not have put me in that role to fail. That just isn't the nature of my Father.

Consider this: We have to see ourselves as God sees us, knowing He has poured an unending supply of His grace over our lives. When God sent Samuel to anoint the king who would reign after Saul, seven of Jesse's sons were brought before him, but none of them was the one He wanted.

I'll bet when David was brought in from tending sheep and anointed king, he wondered how he was going to make the jump from being a shepherd to a monarch. But as 1 Samuel 16:7 recounts, "… For the Lord does not see as man sees; for man looks at the outward appearance, but the Lord looks at the heart."

David, who eventually united the tribes of Israel, is one of the most renowned kings in the Bible. If God moved him from a sheepfold to a palace, think about what He can do for you if you put yourself in His hands.

Knowing Your Worth ... Claiming Your Position

"No one can make you feel inferior without your permission."
~ Eleanor Roosevelt

This simple statement makes a big impact when you understand it. We labor under the weight of other people's opinions, some of whom are not qualified to speak into our lives. All of us have been in the orbit of individuals who are super-critical, some to the point of being mean-spirited. If you can't point to anything constructive they have done with their lives, then those people have no right to give you advice or make you feel less than worthy. Hurt people hurt people.

If you aren't sure of who you are, the guidebook—Bible—God has given us for life on this planet will tell you everything you need to know. He, in His wisdom, has also provided a treasure trove of encouragement for us within its pages. But how do we know He loves us with an everlasting love and that He has inscribed our names on the palms of His hands if we never take the time to dig in and see what His words say about His children?

When my son was much younger, I used to tell him how smart and handsome he was, how much I loved him, and that he had blessed my life. Sometimes he would blush. Other times, he looked at me funny, as though thinking, *she's going overboard again with the mushy stuff.* But through the years, the message sank in. He has turned into a confident young man who knows how I feel about him.

You see, there was a method to my madness. In the same way God gave us His words to tell us who we are to Him, speaking positive words to my son and praying over him before he stepped out each day was a powerful way to impact his life. Another thing I told him was the quote that opens this segment. In different words, of course.

Children can be cruel and it was evident each time he came home and told me he had been called a name or teased for some reason. At those times, I reassured him of what I knew. He was special to both God and his family, and should not allow people to make him feel as if he didn't belong, or as if he was less than anyone else. I reinforced these things because I did not want him to live my experience.

During high school I used to wear jellybean shoes to school because of our budgetary constraints. The name may sound cute and the footwear might have been trendy as casual wear, but I was laughed at for wearing plastic shoes. When I made the transition to sixth form, which is two years of advanced study that come before entering university, and landed a summer job, the first thing I bought was—you guessed it—a pair of regular shoes. Yes, I needed those babies to make me feel I was a normal student.

But God doesn't call us to be normal. He gives each of us assignments that we are to complete in the time we spend on Earth. For too many years, I've made myself smaller to accommodate people who had their own issues and chose unhealthy behavior patterns— microaggression, malicious talk, snide remarks, and gossip that consisted of their version of the truth.

A few years ago, a man I think of as a spiritual father said he believed I had the gift of counsel, and explained what he meant according to the listing in Isaiah 11:1-3.

I considered his words, but didn't attach much weight to them because I didn't see those qualities in myself. Lately, I've come to realize that without me inviting it, people tell me their problems and ask for advice. As yet, no one has told me I've led them astray.

In recent times, I've also been privileged to pray with people over their situations. I don't take that lightly. I've also grown in other areas of my professional and personal life. Until we recognize and nurture the seeds of promise God has placed in us, we won't grasp the fullness of who we are.

As He leads us to new seasons in life and supports us through times of need and times of plenty, we come to realize that He is there showing us where he wants to position us in service to others. Will you allow Him to lead you to where you can be of greatest use to Him?

Consider this: After David was anointed king, a servant of the current ruler, Saul, recommended that the young shepherd be brought in to play the harp. This was to bring Saul peace from the spirit that troubled him. David could have said he was destined for great things and refused. Instead, he did what was asked of him and eventually became Saul's armor bearer.

Despite Saul's eventual jealousy and plans to kill David, the future king never lifted a finger to harm him—even when he had the opportunity. Instead, David followed the path God laid out for him, until he took over the kingdom.

No matter what your situation looks like, think about how you contribute to the lives of those around you and recognize that God has a special place in the Kingdom for you and a plan for your life, too.

Overcoming Famine Mentality

Black people use everything down to the last ounce. This applies to squeezing the toothpaste until there's nothing left in the tube, turning the lotion bottle upside down to drain the last few precious drops, or tilting that perfume bottle to get what's left of a wonderful scent.

Hardships force us not to waste anything simply because we can't afford to do so, but I've noticed a curious thing. When I was a child, there were times when the refrigerator was empty, yet I was never hungry and didn't recognize that the empty shelves meant we had nothing. In my adult life, I can't say I've ever been in a position where my family struggled to find a meal, yet there were other demands that occupied my mind. Bills self-replicated and came back before we could blink. The end of the months seemed to run back to back with days speeding by at a gallop.

When I say God has been good to me, I mean that. Yet, my mind won't stay out of famine mode for long. The challenge is that I like expensive things, but don't always want to spring for the cost. When it comes to software and hardware to enhance my writing life, I spend the money because I believe in a quality product, which I can only produce if I have good equipment.

On a personal level, things look a bit different. Although I'm not struggling, I have the hardest time splurging on myself. My husband and I have spoken about this mind blockage on countless occasions. He chuckles when I bring home shoes and handbags that are not leather.

He'll say something like, "Aren't you tired of buying things that won't last? Isn't it better to buy leather, rather than synthetic material which can't stand a lot of pressure?"

My response usually is, "Do you know how expensive that stuff is?"

He'll shake his head and ask, "Aren't you the one working for that money you're spending on yourself?"

"Yes, but —"

"You have no excuse." This is the part where he points to his closet, and I get another history lesson on the personal items he owns. "Do you know when I bought that pair of shoes?"

By the time we get to this part of the conversation, I'm rolling my eyes, but I get the point. And he's not the only one who has made those kinds of remarks. When my son was small, a coworker said, "Do you know that since you had your son, I've never heard you talk about buying anything for yourself? It's always about him."

"Well, yes. He's growing and needs a constant supply of clothing and school items."

"I understand that, but what about you?"

Her words gave me something to think about, and since then

I've been a little more conscientious about shopping for myself. But the truth is, I tend to outfit myself only when there's an event or if I'm desperately short of clothing. I'm sure you're wondering how much I love myself. But I also know that if you're a mother or wife, you can relate to making sacrifices to be sure your children and husband are fed, clothed, and have the supplies they need.

I've become better over the years because God has blessed me in so many ways. For instance, I started out as a reluctant tither, obviously because I did not trust God. Before you tar and feather me for saying something that sounds like sacrilege, think about the fact that when you are living hand to mouth, tithing feels like a sacrificial stretch.

Yes, it's a mighty test of faith, especially when your church doesn't teach a lot about tithing. God obviously knew we would need some convincing. He says in Malachi 3:10, "Bring all the tithes into the storehouse, that there may be food in My house, And try Me now in this," Says the Lord of hosts, "If I will not open for you the windows of heaven and pour out for you *such* blessing that *there will* not *be room* enough *to receive it.*"

That's a mighty big promise, isn't it? And remember, God cannot lie. Now if only we could unclasp our purse, take a few deep breaths, and focus on His goodness long enough to realize that as a good Father, He will not hesitate to give back to us. I won't lie and say that I'm faithful with tithing. I need to be more consistent. But I urge you not to be like me, because each time I do what I'm supposed to do in gratitude, He rewards me in major and unexpected ways.

If I owe anyone, I don't want it to be Him. Think about it, God has given us everything and all He asks for is a tenth of what we have.

In a funny way, the pandemic has changed the way I spend on myself. For the most part, I've have been working at home two to three days per week in the last year. Before the pandemic, I went to the office every weekday. For a change, payday comes before all the money from the previous check is gone. That's because I haven't been spending as much as I normally do. When I make a shopping trip, I purchase everything in one go for obvious reasons.

The staggering numbers of souls lost in 2020 and 2021 make me realize that life is tenuous. God has blessed me, and if I believe He will continue to supply my needs, what reason do I have to be stingy when it comes to items that will bring me ease and comfort?

When I take the cheapskate route, whether it be shoes or clothing, I am sending a signal to my psyche that I am not worth the money I'm spending. I work hard. If I don't deserve to pamper myself with a little of what I've earned, then I don't know who does. But hey, I'm doing better. I can't be the only one who suffers from this affliction, so if you're in the boat with me, I want to remind you of several things.

You are one of God's precious gems. You are so worth it. Don't allow your circumstances to make you do less than the best for yourself. I don't spend recklessly, but since I don't know when my time on this earth will expire, I've made a commitment to treat myself better. I am resting more, worrying less, reading uplifting material, and keeping positive thoughts. When I awake each day, I thank the Creator for watching over me and my family while we slept and for giving me a new day. I also thank Him for good health and His care and providence.

Consider this: I'm learning to take God at His word and truly appreciate the blessings and gifts He has given me. I encourage you to do the same. His grace will always be more than we deserve, but I urge you to meditate on His words and act as if you know what He knows:

"But you *are* a chosen generation, a royal priesthood, a holy nation, His own special people, that you may proclaim the praises of Him who called you out of darkness into His marvelous light."

Guarding Your Peace

If you're part of a group and you're not growing, it may be time to seek people who have a bigger vision, people you can learn from. When you're the brightest star in your circle, it can be draining.

Some friendships are like prisons without walls. Your energy gets sucked away because you pour so much of it into people who are spinning their wheels with no intention of leaving their current situation for anything better that life has to offer.

I love Joyce Meyer's advice for us to always think about what we're thinking about. We should be conscious of where our thoughts lead us.

Are you forward thinking? Do the people around you speak positively and expect good things to happen to them? Do they have dreams and plans? Do you?

If not, take stock and make some decisions. Are you going to continue on the same journey, or encourage them to take control of their situation? And will you take control of yours? I'm on a path to safeguarding my peace.

Don't think twice about shedding energy vampires from your life. It's sad but true that if you keep company with negative people, you'll be headed in their direction. Sometimes that means staying in a hovering pattern, with no plans to do anything but land in your comfort zone.

I've found it important to guard my spirit. If I allow one negative thought to settle, another follows, and then it's hard to kick them to the curb.

It's okay to be sympathetic to our friends when they need to talk about their problems. We all have them, and need a listening ear. But, it's definitely *not* okay to take on other people's burdens, let their energy seep into you and leave you drained. Guard your spirit.

Life will never be perfect, but happiness isn't found in other people. If that's where you're looking, you'll never find it.

Happiness springs from deep within.

From harmonious relationships.

From finding fulfillment in the things you do.

From discovering your skills and talents.

From getting things done.

From being on the journey with like-minded people.

From rising each day with a plan to work on your dreams and make them reality.

From finding the only source of real peace - The I AM.

None of us will ever be happy 100% of the time. It's not possible, but we can develop an awareness of where our thoughts lead us. More than that, the company we keep is life and death to our dreams.

If your friends can't see your vision and/or understand the direction you're taking, it's time to put them on pause or part company. They're not responsible for your happiness. You are.

Happiness can't be postponed for when you find a husband, have kids, win the lottery, or have a higher-paying job and a better home. Happiness is meant for *now*. Gratitude goes a long way toward helping us see the blessings in our lives. And if we are grateful, it's easy to be content.

If you can't be happy, then be at peace knowing you're doing everything to facilitate the breakthrough you seek. Isaiah 26:3 promises, "You will keep *him* in perfect peace, *whose* mind is stayed *on You*, because he trusts in You."

What a wonderful assurance and promise!

Consider this: David poured out his heart to God, no matter his situation or how he felt. He gave us a rich treasure in the Psalms he wrote because they cover every imaginable emotion. As he cried out to God, we see and understand from his words how his emotions gave way to peace that filled his soul. How much better would we be if we cleaned the gunk out of our system by sharing our thoughts, disappointments, and joys with the Father, who is only a prayer away?

Releasing The Past

Who we are today is the direct result of our past. Nothing is wrong with being influenced by history because our opinions and values come partly from those who raised us. The challenge lies in taking only the good things into the present, while leaving behind as many drawbacks as we can.

Not all of us grew up in a supportive environment, so the critical comments from our childhood and the negative voices in our heads follow us into adulthood. So does the can't-do attitude that leeched into us from those persons who had no idea how to do what they told us we couldn't do.

Jamaica is a matriarchal society. In too many cases, men don't stay in the relationship after they have children. They disappear, leaving women as the sole means of support for their kids. In some instances, frustration sets in and mothers take out their feelings of inadequacy on their kids. They may tell them their fathers are worthless and they will end up just like them. This is not prevalent, but common enough that some individuals end up with self-esteem challenges.

We don't realize that when we speak negative words over our children, we curse them. When they later display the behavior we ascribed to them, we wonder how that happened. The same is true for the deprecating remarks we make about ourselves. It's never a good thing. Our words are powerful. We say things like:

"I'm such a klutz."

"Gosh, I'm such an idiot."

"I'll never be able to get that done."

"Why doesn't anything ever go right for me?"

These may seem like insignificant comments made in the moment, but they are like little markers that determine our actions and box us in, and not in a good way.

When I was about ten years old, I used to write letters to my grandmother, who I visited in the country during the summer months. My mother would supervise this activity, but every time I made a mistake, she'd chuckle and remark on it. Of course, the more she pointed out my errors, the more of them I made. I doubt she understood what she was doing, but it wasn't helping me.

Neither did the adults who asked what I wanted to be when I grew up. With no clue about the future and what would meet me there, my usual response was a shrug or, "I don't know." After being shamed a couple of times, I grabbed a stopgap that satisfied their curiosity.

"A teacher," I'd say. "When I'm older, I want to be a teacher."

That answer removed the spotlight from me, but these encounters also taught me what I wasn't going to do when raising my child. Of course, he's not perfect but I tried not to utter negative words that would occupy any space in his mind and fester—except when he needed to be straightened out.

My experiences are likely very simple in comparison to what you—or someone you know—have been through in childhood. What I'm sure of is that an untold number of persons carry wounds into adulthood that come from incidents that took place when they were young and vulnerable.

As we mature, we go into places of learning and the workplace where we meet other people who have poor interpersonal skills. Our interactions with individuals who do not know how to communicate properly, leave us open to misunderstandings that turn into resentment. And the same goes for our personal relationships. Small issues become big ones and turn into unnecessary arguments.

The years pass and we engage and interact with others, all the while carrying the pinpricks and puncture wounds in our souls from as far back as our childhood. While it's not possible to cast aside our insecurities and the painful memories we suppress, it is helpful to analyze them, see how they've helped and harmed us, fix what we can, seek therapy—if necessary—and cast the rest into the "sea of forgetfulness." Clinging to harmful actions and words never results in anything good. Leave disillusionment and the pain of the past where they belong.

Hit the reset button and step into today as a new version of yourself, having the confidence that God gives in 2 Corinthians 5:17. "Therefore, if anyone *is* in Christ, *he is* a new creation; old things have passed away; behold, all things have become new."

In Revelation 21:5, God reinforces the power He has to change our path and reality when He says, "Behold, I make all things new." These are promises from the Alpha and Omega. Surely, we can believe the Creator of the universe. Challenge yourself to change the way you think, and respond to certain triggers. Stop allowing the past to influence the present.

Consider this: When we accept Christ, we are new creations who do not need to reach into the past for anything that doesn't add value to our existence. How different would your life be, if you stopped pulling scabs off old wounds and allowed them to heal? Grant an immediate exit visa to the people who no longer have the power to hurt you and get them out of your head.

Surrender ... What It Looks Like

I'm so grateful that Jesus is a gentleman and not a gangster. Hold up. Don't get out the whip just yet. Hear me out.

Revelation 3:20 puts it this way: "Behold, I stand at the door and knock. If anyone hears My voice and opens the door, I will come in to him and dine with him, and he with Me."

If He chose to do so, He could railroad us into doing His will. Instead He gives us the freedom to take our path to Him.

We can all identify with adventures we know were not meant for us. Maybe it was a particular group of friends, places we went, or activities that make us shiver when we think about how reckless we were. Our moral compass is formed early in life, but we not only make choices based on our values, we also come under other people's influence. In all of this, God's hand is on our lives as we 'do a Jonah' and go to places He didn't send us.

In the book of the same name, God told Jonah to preach in Nineveh and warn the people that they weren't living right. Instead of doing what he was told, Jonah got on a ship with the intention of going to Tarshish. He decided to be a fugitive from God. The quick and dirty is that a tempest came up and Jonah told the other travelers to throw him overboard because his disobedience caused the storm. They tried hard to save the ship, themselves, and Jonah, but calm returned to the sea when they finally chucked him over the side. Along came a whale that swallowed Jonah, and he was imprisoned in its belly for three days and nights. When he cried out to God, the whale vomited Jonah onto the shore. We won't talk about what state the prophet was in, but the next time God told him what to do, he went without question.

The amazing factoid in this story that's easy to miss is Jonah's faith, although he tried to slide out of the job he'd been given. When the men on the ship were panicking, Jonah told them the sea wouldn't be calm while he was aboard. And he said to them, "Pick me up and throw me into the sea; then the sea will become calm for you. For I know that this great tempest is because of me." (Jonah 1:12) You may wonder why he chose to disobey if he had this level of faith to understand exactly what was happening because of his disobedience.

Putting his adventure into context, God sent him five hundred miles north east, but Jonah headed two thousand, five hundred miles in the opposite direction—literally to the end of the Earth in those days. All the hardship he went though could have been avoided if he did what God told him the first time. On his second go round, he warned the people of Nineveh that God would destroy the city in forty days, and they listened and repented.

He waited outside the city to see if God would destroy it, but grumbled when the plant God shaded him with withered and died, thanks to a worm that attacked it. Instead of being happy that the Ninevites had turned to God, Jonah was disgruntled. He thought God wasted his time because He was merciful and wouldn't have destroyed the people anyway. Even when God spoke to him about the one hundred and twenty thousand souls that were saved because they listened to him, Jonah stayed in his feelings. Isn't it human nature to complain, even when we are the main cause of our misfortune?

We enjoy our youth and settle into raising children and paying bills, all the while concentrating on our struggles and wondering why life has to be so tough. As I've matured, I've looked back and thought about what if I had taken this route instead of that one, and what if I had chosen this person instead of the other one? Would life have been smoother?

Although I was raised to be prayerful, and Catholic schooling reinforced that, the truth is, when I was young and giddy, I didn't ask God anything before I dove in headfirst. Even if He tried to weigh in on the current happenings, I was too busy to hear. When things didn't go as expected, or I was floundering in panic mode, that's the time I showered Him with desperate prayers.

Of course, He saved me from more trouble than I can pinpoint or remember, and I'm grateful He didn't allow me to drown in flood waters of my own making. We all take different routes to our destiny, which is never smooth sailing.

When I look at David's life, it is a testament to God's patience and goodness. David had everything he could possibly want, but one day he saw a woman bathing and decided he couldn't live without her. He found out her name, whose daughter she was, and that she was married. These facts didn't stop him from making moves on her. As if that wasn't bad enough, he got her pregnant.

When Bathsheba's husband returned from fighting in David's army, David decided to cover up what he'd done by sending Uriah home to his wife. But no matter what David did—including making Uriah drunk—the man wouldn't go home. Why? He had a conscience and didn't believe he should enjoy creature comforts while his fellow soldiers didn't have the same privileges.

Since nothing else worked, David formed a fool-proof plan. He decided to send Bathsheba's husband to the front of the next battle, where he was sure to get killed. To quote the Bible, "But the thing that David had done displeased the Lord."

I can think of countless things I've done that haven't been pleasing to God, but perhaps none as dangerous as the story above. The thing is, no matter what we do, or how far we stray, God rescues us from ourselves—as long as we ask for His help.

I'm determined to stop trying to do everything and focus on where I believe I'm meant to go. I would urge you to take inventory and see if you should change anything you're currently doing. See if God is leading you in a particular direction, even if you feel you aren't qualified for whatever you want to do. If He gives you the will to do it, He will make a way and provide the tools you need.

Around five years ago, I started thinking about an inspirational fiction series. I knew it wouldn't be about ordinary people living a good life, because let's face it, we don't always stay on the path to salvation. The series name was fixed in my mind, but other projects kept my attention focused elsewhere. Time went by and I jotted ideas, but I noticed another writer had used the series name I had in mind. It gave me pause, but wasn't a real deterrent. The ideas kept coming, and a cover later caught my eyes. That was the inspiration I needed. One look and I knew what the story would be.

Yet, I was somewhat hesitant because I hadn't written in that genre before, nor had I read many inspirational fiction stories. But I asked for guidance from the Holy Spirit. Eventually, I started writing and three books later, I haven't regretted the time and energy it took to create the three stories in the Virtues & Vices series.

What aspect of your life can you point to that you haven't submitted to God's leading? Is there any dream on your heart that you haven't shared with Him? Are you holding back on taking that first step for fear of failure?

Consider this: Although David is described by God in Acts 13:22 as "a man after My *own* heart, who will do all My will," David followed his desires into a season of disaster, devastation, and repentance, after which his fellowship with God was restored.

We wrestle with our aspirations and try to hide from God when we suspect our desires may not be in His will. And sometimes, we do exactly what God doesn't want us to do, but the way to thrive is to stay connected to Him and ask for His intervention and guidance. He owns our life, so when we go wrong, He will reel us in and walk with us on the journey that's best suited for our growth.

The Hardest Thing To Do: Forgive

Picture this: Joseph, a naïve seventeen-year-old boy shares his dream with his brothers. He tells them they were all binding sheaves in the field and his sheaf stood upright, while theirs gathered around and bowed before his. Can you imagine the conversation?

One brother might have said, "You have got to be joking."

Another might've remarked, "You're out of your mind to think we would bow before you, considering you're the youngest."

He might also have been told, "You'd better go mind the sheep before I take a switch to your backside."

Joseph's father loved him more than all his other children "because he was the son of his old age." That was part of the reason his brothers were jealous.

Joseph didn't learn his lesson. When he had the next big dream, not only did he tell his brothers, but his father as well. In it, he saw the sun, moon, and eleven stars paying him homage.

His father, Jacob, was outraged. You can almost hear him asking, "What is this madness you're dreaming about? Do you think your mother and I, plus your brothers, will come and bow down to the earth before you?" In today's context, he might have said, "Boy, go take a seat somewhere."

This dream made his brothers more jealous.

One day Jacob sent Joseph to see about the welfare of his brothers, who were tending sheep away from home. Despite how his brothers had treated him, Joseph readily did his father's bidding.

But his brothers were still caught up in their feelings and hatched a plot to destroy him. They threw him into a pit. When a group of men on their way to Egypt crossed their path, the brothers changed their plan and sold Joseph into slavery. They chose to cover their actions by deceiving their father into thinking an animal had killed their brother.

They dipped the "coat of many colors" Jacob had made for Joseph into animal's blood, took it home, and showed it as evidence that a four-footed creature had attacked and killed Joseph.

Then the brothers went on their way, living with what they did. Let that sink in.

Think about how awful this whole scene was from Joseph's point of view. The family who was supposed to protect him, betrayed him instead. As the baby, he probably had no idea they were this bitter. He was a dreamer, so half the time he would have missed some of the signals in the airwaves around him. At most, he would have thought they believed he was a nuisance.

As the months and years wore on, Joseph would have come

to understand that his brothers hated him. Why else would they have done something so horrific?

Put yourself in that position. Many of us would not recover from as deep a betrayal as this. We would wallow in our feelings, close ourselves off from those trying to help us, and wonder what we did to deserve not only being enslaved, but later on falsely accused by Potiphar's wife, and thrown into prison, though he hadn't touched her. But like Joseph said when he eventually met his brothers again and saved their lives, "… what you meant for my harm, God meant for my good."

In dealing with his brothers, he broke down on two different occasions. Our expectation would be that he was steeped in hatred. But no, he was happy to be reconciled with his family. I believe this was because he knew God. Joseph did put his brothers through some things, but not from a place of hatred, or to get revenge. This man was a strategist.

We all have suffered hardships. We may have been slighted, robbed, cheated, cheated on, made to feel we were less than, rejected, even hated for reasons we can't understand.

But, we have choices. We can choose to stay in the mire of hate, distrust, and self-pity, or we can take time to assess our situation. It is productive to reflect on the things that have happened to us, why they occurred, how we contributed to them, and whether we could have done anything differently.

When we are hurt, many of us go through the various stages of grieving—denial, anger, bargaining, depression, and acceptance.

Grieving is fine. Resenting the people who hurt us is part of that process. But *staying* in a state of bitterness is not healthy. We put stress on our minds and our bodies when we decide to hate. And yes, it is a decision.

Every time you rehash the incident that threw your life into disarray, check your reaction. Chances are, you're breathing hard, you want to cuss, and your blood pressure has probably spiraled. That is not a healthy state to live in. If you hate or want to harm the person who hurt you, then you haven't forgiven.

Yes, forgiveness is a hard pill to choke down. It takes time. It takes reflection. It takes self-assessment. It takes patience. It means taking your unforgiveness, malice, and the hurt little child inside you to your Heavenly Father. It also means laying yourself at His feet and surrendering to His healing touch. Letting Him pour His Holy Spirit over you like a balm that will soothe your soul.

As I've grown in my walk and relationship with Him, I've learned that forgiveness isn't for the man or woman who hurt my feelings. It's meant for *me*! Making the decision to forgive says I'm willing to travel on a path to a different destination. I can look ahead, knowing I won't make the same mistake again. It's an indication that I understand what Jesus meant when he talked about the torment that would consume the unforgiving servant in Matthew 19:35. "So my Heavenly Father will also do to you if each of you, from his heart, does not forgive his brother his trespasses." He also commanded us to forgive our brothers' sins. Not seven times. Not seventeen times, but seventy times seven.

Yes, that's what's required for peace.

We, also, have hurt other people. Maybe it was something we said, maybe it was some action we didn't realize was selfish or inconsiderate at the time. Maybe something we did made someone feel like less of a person. Perhaps we made an unkind joke about an acquaintance. Or, we cheated an associate out of something they deserved. Like everybody else, we have done many things in life that we do not remember, which is why when we are praying, we ask God to forgive our sins—both known and unknown.

There is nothing quite like realizing you have been carrying a burden of hatred for someone and discovering they had no clue about your feelings. Seems pointless, doesn't it?

We cannot heal by dragging baggage with us from the past that does nothing but weigh us down. Doing that is like lugging suitcases around when we're not traveling. The weight becomes burdensome.

After his ups and downs, Joseph had the power to take revenge on his brothers (Genesis 42:15-20). He put one of his brothers in prison and told the rest to come back with their youngest brother. That's when they discussed the vile thing they had done to Joseph.

I find it amazing that it's at this point we hear about Joseph's reaction on the day they decided to kill him. In verse 21, they talk among themselves. "… We are truly guilty concerning our brother, for we saw the anguish of his soul when he pleaded with us, and we would not hear; therefore this distress has come upon us."

What Joseph didn't know was that Jacob had had another child. I don't believe Joseph's intention was to make his brothers suffer as he had. His actions gave him time to think, plan, and execute the reconciliation with his family.

I don't know about you, but I'm at the stage where I want to be whole, or as healed as possible, coming out of the painful experiences I've endured. When my time is finished on Earth, I want my Lord to say, "Well done, good and faithful servant …"

He will know I'm not perfect but that I tried my hardest to live the way He asked me to, and showed others the same consideration I needed.

Consider this: Imagine what our lives would be like if our Heavenly Father refused to forgive us, the way we refuse to pardon those who have hurt us. Also, think about your stance on forgiveness and how it may be blessing you or holding you back from progressing.

Isn't it better to have peace, instead of the negative emotions you feel when thinking about the person who has hurt you the most? I'd encourage you to be selfish in this matter. Consider your well-being and "… the peace of God, which surpasses all understanding" that He wants to give you. You won't regret it.

Choose joy.

Choose love.

Choose peace of mind.

Choose to forgive.

Restored & Validated

Despite who we have been, who we are now, and who we may become, God has no favorites. He makes no distinction between you and me, and according to scripture, He redeemed me through Jesus' sacrifice not because He had to, but because it's His nature as a loving Father. And so it is for you, as well.

Your Heavenly Father has validated you and charted your life path. Stop running around looking for people to approve of you and give meaning to your life. The fact that you're above ground means God has something for you to do. Your journey is nowhere near complete. Don't waste another day doubting your place in God's plan.

Seek Him and allow Him to help you manifest your goals and dreams. Even if you still don't know where He is leading you, press on until you have clear direction.

Be determined that you will use every drop of the skills and talents He has blessed you with until He calls you home. They exist not only for your development, but to help those in need and those you meet, whose lives you are meant to impact.

When you think like this, you will give Him more of you, and people will see His light shining out of you. No matter what you do, your Heavenly Father will always love you. Honor Him and He will honor you and give you extraordinary favor.

Consider these things: Isaiah 54:10 reminds us of God's everlasting love. "For the mountains shall depart and the hills be removed, but My kindness shall not depart from you, Nor shall My covenant of peace be removed, says the Lord, who has mercy on you." He also declares, "Can a woman forget her nursing child, and not have compassion on the son of her womb? Surely they may forget, yet I will not forget you."

Remember how we talked about God knowing us when we were developing in secret in our mother's womb? Well, He knew us before that. According to Ephesians 1:4-6, "For He chose us in Him before the foundation of the world, that we should be holy and without blame before Him in love, having predestined us to adoption as sons by Jesus Christ to Himself, according to the good pleasure of His will, to the praise of the glory of His grace, by which He made us accepted in the Beloved."

This is excellent news, but if you still have even a remnant of doubt in your mind, remember His words in Jeremiah 31:3 "The LORD has appeared of old to me, *saying:* Yes, I have loved you with an everlasting love; Therefore, with loving kindness I have drawn you."

He truly loves you and knows where you fit into His plan.

Believe Him!

About the Author

National Bestselling Author, J.L. Campbell writes in a range of genres. Campbell, who hails from Jamaica, has penned nearly forty books. She is a certified editor, and book coach. When she's not writing, Campbell adds to her extensive collection of photos detailing Jamaica's flora and fauna. Visit her on the web at amazon.com/author/jlcampbell or www.joylcampbell.com

Connect with me on all networks - Sociatap. https://sociatap.com/JL_Campbell/

FB Page - bit.ly/FacebookJLCampbell

Instagram: bit.ly/InstagramJLCampbell

Twitter: bit.ly/TwitterJLCampbell

Amazon: bit.ly/JLCampbell

Newsletter: bit.ly/JLCampbellsNewsletter

Website: bit.ly/WebsiteJLCampbell

The Merry Hearts Inspirational Series will warm your heart and touch your soul . . .

DNA (Virtues & Vices Book 1)

What can go wrong when an ambitious man accepts a promotion overseas without consulting his wife? A move abroad means physical exams, biometric screenings, and embassy interviews. All normal requirements, or they would be, if she didn't believe they might stir a hornet's nest. Whether her marriage will survive a shocking revelation, and her faith withstand a trial by fire, is anyone's guess. ***DNA is inspirational fiction with a focus on marriage.

Russ folded his arms around Amoy and struggled to meet her eyes in the mirror. "Don't look at this move as my job turning things upside down. Think of it as an adventure."

She exhaled hard, turned in his arms, and laid both hands on his chest. "Our life is in Jamaica. The boys are in a good school. Their family is here and—"

"Em." He pressed a finger to her lips to stem her words. "I'm not asking you to pull up roots forever. It will be for five years at most. *If* it happens."

Her fingers traveled the length of his white tie before she stood on tiptoes and kissed him. Amoy avoided his gaze as she asked, "Can we talk about this later?"

"You're right. Later is better," he whispered in her ear. "Maybe if we enjoy some extra special time together, you'll change your mind."

She chuckled and patted his bearded jaw. "It'll take a lot more than *that* to change my mind."

"You love the way I love you." His voice dropped to a husky note and he wriggled his brows. "I know everything you like."

That made her grin and slip her arms around his neck. "I may have some news for you, but it'll keep," she said.

"Okay, but can you give me a hint?" He pecked her forehead and held her away from him. He couldn't read the light in her eyes as she moved her head slowly from side to side. "Nope."

"Later then." He looked at his watch. "Let's go. I don't want to be late."

"Let me tell the boys goodnight." She stepped into her shoes, which brought her close to his height—just over six feet.

Amoy looked good in a cream strapless dress that left her shoulders bare. The fabric hugged her curves, which made Russ want to stay home and make love to her. That was wishful thinking because he couldn't miss the awards ceremony being hosted by his employer, Saunders & Royes Distributors.

As Amoy shrugged into a jacket that matched her dress, a twinge of guilt pricked Russ. He'd posed the idea of them migrating as something that might happen, when he'd already agreed to take the position in Miami. Since the start of the year, he'd been flying back and forth frequently. Nine months in, the constant traveling had worn on him. He thought he'd grown used to the demands of the job, but he was wrong.

Amoy applied lipstick, then rushed out of the room with her drop earrings sailing in the air. Behind her, she left a trail of Volupté—a fruity-flowery-woodsy perfume, her signature scent.

Their live-in helper, Miss Sarah, would watch the boys tonight. Russell, Jr. and Troy liked and respected her, and were already in their room getting ready for bed since they had school the following day.

Russell had been with them for the last hour so he wouldn't disturb their bedtime ritual. He spent so much time at the office that the boys were always excited to see him. This wasn't the way he wanted things to be and was far from the original goals he'd set for his life, but he had to live up to his professional responsibilities.

He looked at himself in the mirror, dusted the shoulders of his black shirt, then got his jacket out of the closet. At the threshold, he flicked the light switch and shut the door behind him.

Amoy had left the bedside lamp on to avoid them returning to total darkness.

In the living room, Miss Sarah sat watching the evening news.

Amoy came into the room from the opposite passage, slipping her phone inside her purse.

From the sofa, Miss Sarah grinned at them. "I hope di two of yuh enjoy unooself."

"We will," Amoy said, walking toward Russ.

Miss Sarah's comment made him smile. She'd left the parish

of St. Elizabeth three decades ago and still spoke as if she got off the country bus last week. Her broken English didn't bother him anymore but, at first, he feared the boys would start speaking like her. He needn't have worried. They understood Patois as well as English and knew when to use both.

Amoy reached to the carport ahead of him, while he mused that her womanly curves were very much at odds with her baby face. Even now, she didn't look a day over twenty-five.

He unlocked the Ford Escape and switched on the engine remotely, then helped Amoy get in. She sat, swung her legs inside, and blew him a kiss.

As she settled in the seat, he stepped back. "I'm beginning to think we shouldn't go out tonight. That dress has me distracted."

Amoy looked at him through the hair she'd combed to one side of her face. "You better stop joking and get in. If you don't turn up, your boss will blame me and you won't tell him it's your fault we didn't show."

Laughing, Russ laid his jacket on the back seat of the SUV. "You're right about that."

When he got behind the wheel, he studied Amoy. She'd gone from Amoy to Moy and he'd shortened that to Em, over time. They'd been married for eight years and he loved her as much today as he had at the start of their relationship.

"So, are you getting an award?" Amoy asked while fiddling with the radio.

"I doubt it, but they may mention the promotion they've offered me."

"Mmm."

Amoy turned the radio dial until she found a station playing love songs.

As they pulled out of the yard and the gate closed behind them, Russ said a prayer all would go well this evening. He was hopeful that by the time they got back home, Amoy would have softened her stance on the matter of them moving.

He had another week on the island before he had to return to the Miami office, and didn't want to spend it fighting. Relocating would make things easier for him. His mother lived in Miami and her health was deteriorating. He'd rest easier knowing he was close by in case of any emergency. Mama was stubborn, but was now living with his sister, which meant he didn't have to worry too much. They weren't close, but Tanya saw to their mother's needs with financial assistance from Russ.

His mind moved to a different track as he drove across town, dodging taxi drivers. Their cars were usually chockfull of people and they always seemed to be in a hurry. They made driving in Kingston hazardous. Route taxi drivers often ignored traffic signals because of indiscipline and the need to maximize their income by making as many trips as possible.

While he navigated through the streets, Russ tried to figure out something special he could do with the boys before he went overseas again. Whether he'd get to do that was anybody's guess.

He turned the SUV into the hotel parking lot. The awards dinner was being hosted at one of Kingston's finest hotels. Russ admired that about the company. They treated their employees well and didn't stint on benefits and events.

On the way through the elegant lobby with Amoy on his arm, Russ acknowledged staff members also on their way to the ballroom. They didn't have much time to socialize because in less than twenty minutes, an executive assistant herded them from the bar in the outer area through to the ballroom.

Russ and Amoy were seated with the company executives at a table for ten near the stage. As Amoy chatted with the directors' wives, Russ couldn't help but be proud of her. She fit in everywhere she went and always hit the right notes, no matter the occasion.

When the small talk subsided and the emcee made the opening remarks, Russ sent up another prayer. If everything went his way, nobody would spill anything they shouldn't before he had a chance to win Amoy to his way of thinking.

Their dinner of garlic shrimp in coconut milk and herbed chicken breasts was served with pasta and steamed vegetables.

Phillip Saunders, the CEO, sat on Russ's left and kept up an unending conversation over dinner, while Russ stayed on tenterhooks the entire time.

The women talked about their children, the best schools, and a spa facility that opened recently.

After the waiters delivered assorted cheesecake bites for dessert, the music tapered into silence, and the emcee took the stage.

"Don't forget our appointment," Russ murmured in Amoy's ear. "I can't wait."

Amoy bit back a grin, then whispered, "Behave yourself."

He sat up and nodded to his wife's boss, who gave him an approving smile then turned her attention to the man at the podium.

The awards presentation went on for a half-hour. Those who received awards had worked for Saunders & Royes from five to fifteen years.

Russ had only been with the company for six years, but advanced rapidly, earning three promotions. He was proud of the work he'd done and happy with the steps he'd made. The job provided generously for his family, and that was important to him. His people were nowhere near as privileged as Amoy's and it was a point of pride to be able to take good care of her and their children.

He believed part of what troubled Amoy was that she didn't want to give up her job. She worked for her father's medical supply company and was used to earning her own money. If the family shipped out, she'd be a homebody—at least for a while.

Russ shelved his thoughts when the emcee called his name. As he walked to the stage, he nodded to acknowledge the applause of staff members and well-wishers. He accepted the crystal memento with the company's logo. He'd been voted the most innovative manager by the staff.

Phillip stood beside Russ while he gave his thank you speech. When he finished, Phillip clapped him on the back and leaned toward the mic. "Russ is not only full of great ideas that have put the company's name out there, he continues to work hard to make Saunders & Royes the best production and distribution company in the hemisphere."

He paused and Russ swallowed hard, hoping Phillip wouldn't say much more. As he continued, a weight dropped on Russ's shoulders.

"I'm pleased that we can expect bigger and better things in the months to come as Russ has accepted the position of Regional Manager and will be based in our Miami office starting in November."

Russ kept his cool, but couldn't help the way his gaze darted to the table where Amoy sat a few feet from the stage.

A slight smile curved her lips, but her eyes smoldered. When she looked directly at him, one of her brows cocked ever so slightly. Amoy picked up her wine glass and sipped, still staring at him.

Meanwhile, Russ's stomach plunged to his leather Oxford shoes.

Guilt is a bitter enemy when you sacrifice one precious gift for another.

Dane's two-year-old daughter is the center of his world, and doubly precious because of her health challenges. When he discovers a son from a previous relationship, his world implodes. No matter what path he takes, everything he holds dear is at stake, and life will never look the way it did before tragedy knocked at his door.

***Sacrifice is inspirational fiction with a focus on marriage.

"Thanks, but no thanks."
Amoy's refusal six months ago still haunted Dane daily.

Her response to his proposal had been stoic, which could have fooled him into believing she was fine. That's what she wanted him to think. The pain in her eyes had been like a gut punch, which hit especially hard because he was going through his own issues.

Dane's conscience tried to tell him that his refusal to acknowledge her son was punishment, but he brushed it aside. Though his intellect knew better, his heart said something else.

A bald man in pale blue scrubs stopped in front of the seats where Dane had settled next to Sophie. Her hand crept into his and he squeezed it, more for her reassurance than his. No matter how the hospital dressed up the building with plants and comfortable furniture, it was hard to forget why there were there.

"Mr. and Mrs. Whitby?"

Dane sat up. "That's correct."

"I'm Dr. Lopez. We've stabilized Nyla but I can't stress enough the importance of doing the next surgery as soon as possible." He paused and cleared his throat. "The longer we delay, the more likely it is that she'll develop severe complications."

"We understand." Dane glanced at Sophie then back at the doctor. "We'll get in touch with Dr. Millwood."

The doctor with an olive complexion and silky, jet-black hair filled the awkward pause while rubbing the back of his neck. "That's for the best."

"Thank you," Dane said, as Sophie swiped tears off her cheeks.

This endless cycle of hospital visits and consultations with Nyla's cardiologist had been their lot since her birth two years ago. After a routine doctor's visit during Sophie's pregnancy, their obstetrician had ordered a fetal echocardiogram. He relayed the bad news a few days later that their baby had a heart defect.

They prayed their way through the remaining four months and hoped for the best.

After Sophie delivered the baby, their relief was short-lived. Their joy turned to ashes when the medical team wore concerned expressions and went into a whispered conversation just out of their hearing.

"When can we see her?" Sophie asked, cutting into Dane's memories.

"Another half-hour to forty-five minutes," the doctor replied.

"How soon can we take her home?" Dane asked, praying this wouldn't be an extended stay.

"We'll be in a better position to say tomorrow." A slight smile curved the man's lips. "She's a fighter so I imagine it will be sooner, rather than later."

Dane acknowledged his comment with a nod.

When the doctor walked away, Dane angled his body to face Sophie. "I'll get some things and be back here within an hour. Will you be okay?"

Sophie sniffed and wiped her swollen eyes. "Make sure you bring her bumble bee."

Her request pulled a faint smile from him. "She wouldn't allow me into her room if I didn't."

The combination support cushion and plush toy was Nyla's favorite, next to a beige bunny with super-long ears that Nyla had named Harold or 'Harra' in her baby speech. Her grandfather's name was Harold, and he was always delighted when Nyla pointed to him and the rabbit and said his name.

"Try not to worry too much," Dane warned as he stood.

Sophie's smile was shaky. "I'll try."

"Say a prayer instead."

She rubbed her forehead and got to her feet. "I think I'll go for a walk and get a cup of coffee or something."

Gently, he said, "Then you won't sleep for a week. We can't have that."

She fell in step with him, and he cupped her elbow.

"I'm just trying to stay alert for when Ny wakes," she said.

He guided her to one side of the corridor and stopped. "What I don't want you to do is stay awake all night watching her. As you're always telling me, 'God's got this.'" He tipped her chin toward him. "Prove to me that you believe what you say and rest when you're tired."

She smiled, but the gesture didn't light her eyes. Tears flooded them again, and he drew her into a hug. In times like these, he wished he knew what to do to heal Sophie's hurt. She blamed herself for Nyla's condition, and telling her that she wasn't at fault didn't make a difference. Sophie had convinced herself that having a child at thirty-eight was partly the cause of their daughter's condition. They both knew that many women opted to delay having children until later in life, but Sophie still didn't ease up on herself.

Maybe this has more to do with you than her.

He stifled that thought and allowed Sophie to hold on to him as long as she needed. He smoothed her short hair and dropped a kiss on her ear. When she stood back, she looked better. Her melanin-rich skin still glowed, and her eyes were brighter. He gave Sophie a handkerchief and slid an arm around her. "Tell you what we'll do. I'll bring you a sandwich and something to drink from home. You haven't eaten all day."

She sighed, and he kissed her softly. "I'll be back as soon as I can."

"Okay. I'll call if anything changes."

He left her standing inside the hospital's sliding doors and strode to the parking lot. When he sat inside his Audi Q7 SUV, he gripped the wheel for a few seconds and settled his thoughts before driving off. They lived in walking distance, but he'd been away from his home office when Sophie called to say she'd taken Nyla to the hospital.

Within five minutes, he stood outside their two-story townhouse. Their decision to purchase had to do, in part, with proximity to the best children's hospital in Orlando. Their lives revolved around Nyla's illness and they were now used to that being the case.

On his way inside, his cell phone rang. He fumbled in his haste to pull it out of his pocket, but the call wasn't from Sophie. His heart settled into its regular rhythm as he answered, "Hey, Steve, what's up?"

His friend's deep baritone matched his strapping physique. "Just checking in with you to see if you'll be at men's fellowship tonight."

As he ran up the stairs, Dane said, "Won't make it. Ny's in the hospital again."

"I'm sorry to hear that. I'll tell the guys and we'll say a word for you and the family."

"Thanks, man."

Each month, he only made the Wednesday evening gathering once or twice, but enjoyed the rapport with the men from the Divine Mission Worship Center.

He called his mother to update her, then slid the phone into his pocket and went into Nyla's room to gather the items Sophie requested. Dane lifted the three-in-one comfort bumble bee and squeezed it to his chest. The toy carried a powdery scent he identified with Nyla. On his way past the chest-of-drawers, their family portrait stopped him, and he picked it up. In it, Nyla was four months old, but looked more like a newborn.

One of the symptoms of her condition—Hypoplastic Left Heart Syndrome—was breathlessness, and Nyla's struggle tired her easily. That meant she didn't feed enough to gain weight. Aside from sticking with the recommended high-calorie formula and waiting for the next surgery, they couldn't do much else at the time. Many nights, they stood over Nyla, hoping the bluish tinge to her skin would fade to a healthy shade of brown.

Dane stroked her cheek through the glass, wishing it was within his power to switch places with Nyla. Their little girl was the best of both her parents. The perfect expression of their love for each other. He replaced the picture and rushed to his bedroom to get Harold. Because of Sophie's illness, they hadn't removed her crib from their room.

He went to the closet and retrieved the bag that stayed packed in case they had to remain overnight at the hospital. This time, he avoided looking at the photo that captured Nyla at six months.

Sophie's reluctance to go ahead with Nyla's second surgery had almost ended in tragedy. That time, the hospital was home to their little girl for nearly two weeks. He closed the door on the past and left the room. At the bottom of the stairs, he took a detour to the kitchen.

Sophie stuck to self-imposed rules that dictated what she put into her body, so he was limited in what he could buy at a fast food restaurant. Plus, the close proximity to the children's hospital meant going in the opposite direction, which didn't make sense.

While he heated the latest veggie-mush Sophie had taken to eating, he got a bottle of coconut water from the freezer.

He dropped his tie on the stool at the counter and fixed the sandwich, wishing he hadn't skipped lunch today. The Lord knew he was tired of these frequent hospital trips, but he wouldn't complain aloud. Especially not after the disgraceful way he'd acted with Amoy months ago.

He'd asked God to forgive him. Now if only he could forgive himself for disowning the son he didn't know he'd fathered.

Women. Money. Parties. Dominic Whitehorn's life revolves around these staples until his business fails and he wakes up to the reality that he's broke, and living in a foreign land. Financial ruin isn't his only challenge. The woman he's interested in believes he's a lightweight, and another claims he's the father of her baby.

Ashley Dennis knows Nick is a troubled soul because she's been there. They make an unlikely couple, but will her example and conviction be the catalyst he needs to turn his life around?

***Dominic's Pride is inspirational fiction with a focus on family and relationships.

What day is it? Nick searched his mind and came up with Thursday.

In the hazy early morning light, he looked at the clock on the bedside table. Half past seven.

The woman he'd slept with last night tugged at the nape of his neck, pulling his face toward hers. Groaning, she grazed his cheek with her lips.

Nick shook his head, turned off by her breath and the sour taste in his mouth.

Who the hell was she and how had she gotten into his bed?

He'd had way too much to drink and remembered next to nothing of what happened after he got home. A blurry picture of them leaving the night club hand in hand and waving down a cab was all he had to rely on to refresh his memory.

Nick sat up, clutching his head. Of all the things he'd done in recent times, this was the worst. He hoped he'd used a condom, but his brain cells refused to cooperate and give him a clear picture of what took place.

She shifted on the bed and ran one finger up his back to lure him back into the warm bed, but he was now wide awake and conscious of everything he'd forgotten.

"Are you all right?" she asked when he didn't respond.

He grunted and inhaled deeply, relieved his brain function had returned to normal. Kylie. A woman he met a grand total of ten hours ago. This time, he'd gone over the line.

This new lapse happened because he was under stress, which he didn't want to face at this hour of the morning, but he couldn't escape his thoughts.

His head throbbed harder. The student loan payment had left

him struggling, and the rent on his apartment was due in another couple of days. He didn't look forward to making that call to Jamaica to ask his father for money, nor did he want to deflect Dad's arguments about him going home.

Nick wasn't interested in an entry-level job at one of their hardware outlets. His brother, Marlon, who was almost thirty-nine, acted like a man ten years older. The thought of him lording it over Nick made him sick.

Kylie slid one finger into the waistband of his shorts, bringing Nick back to his current predicament. Over his shoulder, he said, "I've got to be at the office early today, so use the bathroom first."

"So this is how it's going to be?"

Her high-pitch irritated Nick, and he sat sideways on the bed. "How what's going to be?"

She glared at him, pouting at the same time. Her weave was now a huge clump of curls with blonde streaks. She resembled a giant lollypop, but the look she gave him was anything but sweet. "Fine, be like that."

She flounced into the bathroom and shut the door.

In her absence, he gathered her clothes, changed the sheets, and flipped the switch on the kettle. Then, he laid his clothing across the bed and dropped his shoes on the bedside carpet.

Kylie came back wrapped in a towel.

"Let yourself out," he said on the way past her.

She didn't answer, and he prayed she'd be gone by the time he finished his shower.

He made sure it was a quick one, but when he poked his head into the living room, Kylie stood in the kitchen nook, sipping from a coffee mug.

At least she was back in her clothes, which was a good sign.

Books By J.L. Campbell

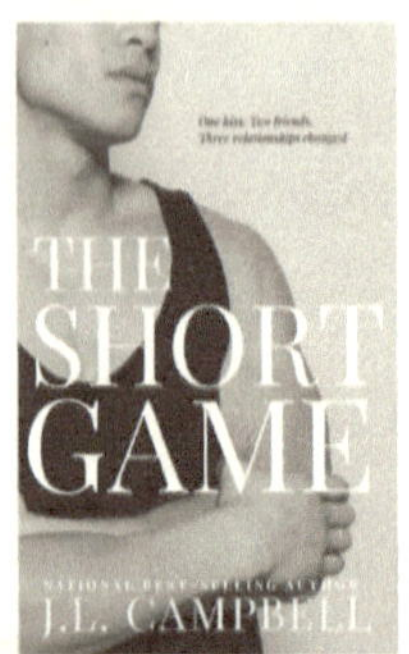

Connect with J.L. Campbell
www.joylcampbell.com

Books By J.L. Campbell

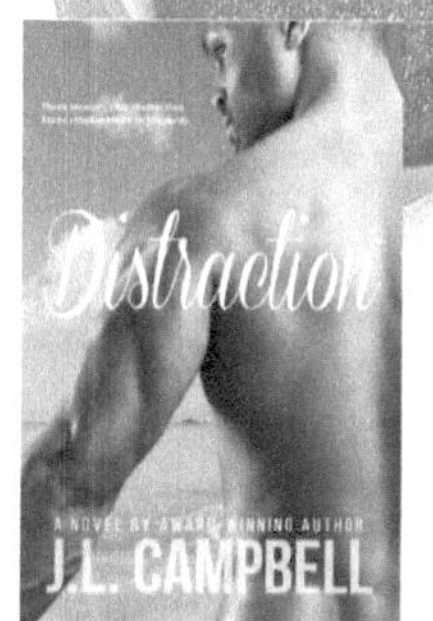

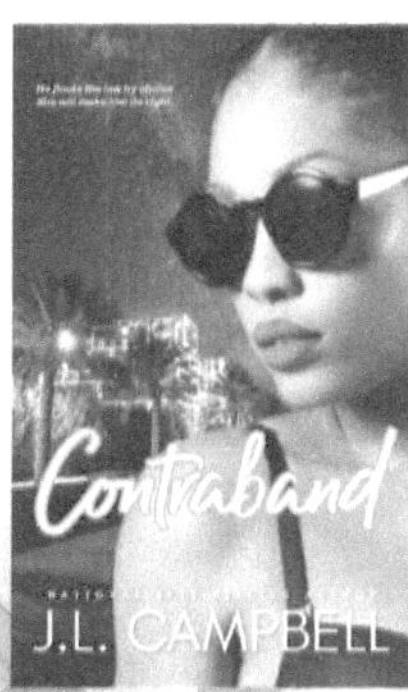

Connect with J.L. Campbell
www.joylcampbell.com

Books By J.L. Campbell

Connect with J.L. Campbell
www.joylcampbell.com